MOONSHINING

in the Great Smoky Mountains

BY
Daniel S. Pierce

Great Smoky Mountains Association is a nonprofit organization
which supports the educational, scientific, and historical programs
of Great Smoky Mountains National Park. Our publications are an
educational service intended to enhance the public's understanding
and enjoyment of the national park. If you would like to know more
about our publications, memberships, and projects, please contact:
Great Smoky Mountains Association
P.O. Box 130
Gatlinburg, TN 37738
(865) 436-7318
www.SmokiesInformation.org

CONTENTS

3

INTRODUCTION

White lightning, corn squeezins', mountain dew, white mule, splo', white dog, moonshine! Whatever you call it, no other product is more iconic and more associated with traditional life in the Great Smoky Mountains than illegally distilled, un-aged, white corn liquor. Seemingly no popular image of life in this mountain region—whether in art, in print, on film, or in song—is complete without the presence of a one-gallused moonshiner, a 40-gallon copper pot still, and a stoneware jug marked XXX.

Almost since the day Abraham Lincoln signed into law a federal excise tax on distilled spirits in 1862, moonshine and the Smokies moonshiner have been steeped in myth and lore, at turns sensationalized, demonized and romanticized. The sensationalizers have included a national press, eager to sell papers and magazines in the late 19th century, addicted to tales of shootouts and outright war between illegal producers and revenue agents. Short story writers and novelists of the local color movement in the same era sought to attract readers by depicting the people of the Great Smoky Mountains as exotic. Early filmmakers built on those images and themes and cartoonists, television producers, documentary filmmakers, and reality TV show creators picked up where the others left off producing a continual stream of lurid moonshiner stereotypes up to the present day.

Advocates of temperance, alcohol prohibition, and regional reform tended to condemn and demonize moonshiners. In the late 19th century many Protestants in the Smokies, particularly Baptists and

5

Methodists, moved to a hardcore teetotal stance on alcohol consumption and manufacturing making the moonshiner public enemy number one. Home missionaries, many of whom came from New England to uplift "depraved" mountaineers, and local town elites who sought to bring industry, stable habits, and improvement to the region, supported calls for prohibition and saw blockaders as representative of the worst type of folks in the region and their ilk an impediment to progress. Of course many federal law enforcement and revenue agents who exchanged gunfire with the region's moonshiners did not look fondly on the purveyors of illegal liquor either and often promoted these negative stereotypes.

As moonshine has become less physically present in the region in recent years, the trend has been to romanticize the life of the moonshiner as a modern-day Robin Hood, an outlaw who defies the oppressive forces of "guvmint" and simply exercises his God-given right to make a little liquor, or to view the moonshiner as an essentially harmless, yet colorful character along the lines of a Popcorn Sutton. The urge to romanticize moonshine and moonshine making is especially powerful among movie and television producers and country music and bluegrass songwriters and performers. In very recent years, that trend toward romanticizing has been picked up by an ever-increasing number of producers of legal moonshine, who have found a powerful market in nostalgia for a supposed lost era of mountain craftsman distillers.

My goal in writing this book is to try to avoid all three of these trends; indeed my hope is to humanize the moonshiner. It is important to understand this regional phenomenon as the product not only of individual choices, but also of deep-seated cultural, economic, and social conditions that created a complex and shifting historical context in which the moonshiners plied their trade. For some residents of the Smokies, making moonshine provided tangible benefits particularly in providing ready cash in a generally cash-poor society. Many farmers in the region paid their tax bills, mortgages, and store bills; bought shoes and school books for their children and new land or homes for themselves; started businesses; and realized genuine benefits from their "ill-gotten" gains. Others made the product because their families always made it, some because they loved to drink it, and still others because they loved the adrenalin-rush of the cat-and-mouse game played between moonshiners and revenuers.

At the same time, it should not be forgotten that many of these same individuals paid real costs for their participation in the moonshine business. They spent time away from spouses and children in jail or prison, and lived stressful lives constantly looking over their shoulders. Their lives were often marred by violence, and they found themselves pulled into illegal and immoral activities in ways they probably never imagined before they took to blockading.

The illegal liquor business also had its positive and negative impacts on communities in the Smokies. Moonshiners supported and injected lots of cash into local businesses from country stores to automobile dealerships and provided paying work that helped keep talented individuals in the community. The proceeds from illegal liquor provided financial support to build and maintain churches, schools, and other local institutions. But communities also paid a price when residents elevated such illegal activity and almost expected participation as normal activity. It became very easy in many places in the Smokies to promote and tolerate other forms of illegal and abusive behavior which took their toll on family and community life. Fear of informers could make communities inordinately suspicious of outsiders and the outside world and dangerously inward looking. While often the products of exaggeration and stereotype, many communities in the region still have a reputation for violence and illegal activity that is difficult to transcend.

To be honest, I am perhaps one of the unlikeliest individuals to write a book on moonshine. My dad was a Southern Baptist preacher and I doubt that he ever took a drink of alcohol of any kind and he regularly preached against it. If anything, my mother is more of a teetotaler than he was. While I personally take a more Biblical approach to the consumption of alcohol—after all, Jesus turned water into wine and that was characterized as a good thing—I'm not much of a drinker myself.

That said, the subject of moonshine is one that has attracted me for a number of years. I have lived near the Great Smoky Mountains for much of my life, did a Ph.D. dissertation and later a book on the history of the region, and have long been fascinated with the people who live here. Subsequently, I took an interest in the history of NASCAR which unavoidably led me into the world of illegal liquor. For me, the story of moonshine is a story of how people of little, and often worsening, means tried to find ways to cope with the difficulties of life. To do so, they looked to their cultural roots, to their environment, and to the vagaries of the market. For many individuals and families, making moonshine, for at least part of their life, was a logical act. Again, some benefitted from their activities and some became locked in a downward spiral that in the long run worsened their prospects, scarred their families, and skewed their communities. Indeed, I hope the reader will come to understand that while the story of moonshine in the Smokies contains much that is sensational, downright demonic, and even romantic, it is most often a story of imperfect human beings trying their best to survive and even thrive in difficult circumstances in a challenging environment.

CHAPTER 1
TURNING CORN INTO CASH

Buried in their wagon under the spinning wheel, a few pieces of furniture, a washtub, and possibly a fiddle, many of the earliest European inhabitants of the Great Smoky Mountains brought along a copper pot distillery. Many were of Scots-Irish ancestry, hardy settlers with a long history of distilling grains and fruits into alcohol. Indeed, the very word whiskey derives from the Gaelic word *usquebaugh*—generally translated as water of life—and the earliest records of Anglo-Saxon invaders of Scotland noted the commonality of spirit making among Celtic peoples. For the peoples of the Celtic fringe (Scotland, Ireland, and Wales) whiskey production and drinking were integral parts of social, economic, and political life well before they crossed the Atlantic. In the words of moonshiner Luke Doolin, the main character in the B-movie classic *Thunder Road*, making liquor was part of the tradition of his ". . . daddy, grandaddy, his daddy before him clear back to Ireland."

As they migrated to America, Europeans adapted their cultural practices to new surroundings. As early as the 1620s, English settlers in Virginia learned to distill the common grain of Native Americans, maize or Indian corn, into whiskey. Anglican missionary Captain George Thorpe wrote to a friend back in England that he had set up a distillery on the banks of the James River and learned "to make so good a drink of Indian corn as I protest I have divers times refused to drink good strong English beer and chosen to drink that." By the time the Scots-Irish began arriving in droves in the 1720s, making corn liquor was a common practice in England's American colonies. As historian W. J. Rorabaugh observed, "The success of the whiskey industry was due, in part, to the fact that many Scottish, Irish, and Scotch-Irish grain distillers had immigrated to America during the last quarter of the eighteenth century. . . . When these Irish and Scots settled on the American frontier, they found conditions favorable for the exercise of their talents: plentiful water, abundant grain, and ample wood to fuel their stills." By the 1810s, when white settlers began trickling into the Great Smoky Mountains, the craft of producing corn liquor was well-established among backcountry residents.

While distilling corn into whiskey involves few ingredients and requires little in the way of equipment, it is a complicated process that requires experience, patience, and skill. Practically anyone can make liquor, but it takes talent to make good liquor. As the author of a classic work on moonshining, Joseph Earl Dabney observed, "Making corn whiskey, as anyone in the Appalachians will tell you, is an art, not merely boiling mash and running it through a still. The secret is getting the right ingredients in those mash barrels." Or as moonshiner Short Stanton of Greene County, Tennessee put it more colorfully, "It's like a woman making biscuits. If she don't know how to make them over thar in the mixing bowl, when she puts them in the pan, they ain't no count."

While there are many variations on the traditional craft of making corn liquor, the basic process is pretty standard. The first step—and one of the reasons the Smokies became a premier location for the production of liquor—is to locate a dependable source of water. "Soft" water that contains few trace minerals is generally regarded as best for making good whiskey and most of the creeks and streams of the Smokies—with its base of hard, metamorphic rock—contain "soft" water. With an average of over 80 inches of rainfall per year at higher elevations, the Smokies provide a plentiful source as well. Early settlers learned to examine the plant life along streams to determine whether the water was "soft" or "hard." The presence of yellow root or horsemint indicated that the water was soft, while touch-me-nots were signs of hard water. Whiskey makers consider the water flowing over relatively iron-free limestone as the

The Great Smoky Mountains are drenched by up to seven feet of annual rainfall which runs off in thousands of miles of pure, sparkling streams.

absolute best for making whiskey, so the area in and around Cades Cove was especially prized for whiskey making.

After finding a good source of water, the next step is to make the mash. While recipes differ, most traditional mash is a mixture of ground corn—white corn is generally preferred—corn malt, and water. Corn malt is produced by taking whole kernels of corn, soaking them in water for a day, draining the water but keeping the corn damp for three to four days until two-inch sprouts emerge, drying the sprouted corn, and finally grinding it in a mill. Some makers used rye or barley malt instead, but the ready availability of corn made it the most common malt. The corn meal is then mixed with the malt and hot water in a barrel or wooden box and left to sit for five to ten days to ferment. The mash will bubble during this process and produce a foamy layer on top known as the cap.

When this "sour mash" stops bubbling and the cap disappears, the resulting "beer" (about 10% alcohol) is ready for distillation. Most commonly, early whiskey producers in the Smokies used a ten- to forty-gallon copper pot still. Copper has long been the preferred metal for distilling as it is light, tough, conducts heat well and evenly, does not leach metals into the alcohol, and does not corrode. The beer is poured into the still and a fire started in a stone furnace built around the still to contain and evenly spread the heat. Once the beer reaches the boiling point of alcohol at 173 degrees Fahrenheit, the still cap is sealed on top (usually with malt paste) and distillation begins. The alcohol vapor produced from boiling the mash rises to the still cap where it escapes through a coiled copper tube run through a mountain stream or a barrel containing cold, running water. The cool water condenses the vapor back into liquid which drips through a clean cloth containing charcoal to filter impurities.

For the traditional Smoky Mountains craft whiskey maker, however, this is not the end, but just the first run of "singlings" which contain impurities such as fusel oil and is of relatively low alcohol content. The distiller must now pour out the leftover mash residue, known as "slops," and thoroughly clean the still. Slops which have only been run a few times can be emptied back into new mash to help speed the fermentation process. Once they are spent they can be fed to livestock—hogs love it.

The singlings are run back through the still, filtered, and once again trickle into a container. The distiller checks the proof of the liquor by periodically running some of the product into a small bottle known as a proofing vial. Experienced makers can judge proof with a quick shake of the vial and observing the "bead." The size of the bubbles which form—the bead—and the speed that they dissipate, or "flash off," indicates the proof. As one liquor maker explained it, "If it's high proof—say 115 to 120—a big bead will jump up there on top when you shake it. If the proof is lower, the bead goes away faster and is smaller. Hand a mountain man a pint of whiskey and the first thing he'll do is shake it. A true bead will stop half in the likker and half out on top."

Another way of judging proof is by watching the stream of alcohol coming out of the worm. At 160 proof, the stream becomes twisted and spirals into the catch container. This part of the run produces what distillers refer to as the "high shots." Watching the stream also lets the

ALCOHOLIC BEVERAGE
PROOFS

Beer   Wine   Brandy   Spirits   Moonshine

maker know when the run is done, when the liquor "breaks at the worm" and is producing low-proof "backings." Backings are collected separately and either run with the next batch of mash or mixed with the high shots to lower the proof.

Distillers pour this "doubled and twisted" whiskey in a large container called a tempering tub where they mix the liquor from several runs and lower the proof to the desired level, usually around 100-110, by adding backings and/or water. In the 18th and 19th centuries, whiskey makers in the Smokies would then transfer the product to stoneware jugs or into charred oak kegs for aging.

While corn liquor was the most common product made by distillers in the Smokies during this period, they also produced brandy from local fruit. The process for making brandy is pretty much the same as for producing whiskey, with the mashed fruit—known as pomace— placed in barrels with corn or rye malt to ferment and then being double run through a still. Brandy commanded a much higher price than corn

13

liquor, so distillers made it at every opportunity. As one producer put it, "Just anybody can't afford brandy. Mostly for judges and lawyers." Indeed, much of the sizeable apple crop in the Smokies went to make some type of alcoholic beverage from hard cider to distilled apple brandy. Producers also used peaches, plums, grapes, elderberries, and even maypops (the fruits of wild passion-flower). In the 1840s, Moses Proctor planted a small peach orchard in Hazel Creek for the sole purpose of making peach brandy.

Consumption of alcohol had a prominent place in the life and culture of the region. As Horace Kephart observed, "As a rule, the mountain people have no compunctions about drinking." While liquor was generally only consumed by adult males in public, women, children, and even babies drank it in the home. Kephart reported seeing "undiluted spirits drunk, a spoonful at a time, by a babe that was still at breast, and she never batted an eye." It must be remembered that throughout much of the 18th and 19th centuries in the United States—despite the growth of a national temperance movement in the 1830s, '40s, and '50s in the towns and cities—there was little social or religious stigma to drinking hard liquor. By 1830, per capita annual consumption of liquor exceeded five gallons nationally.

Aunt Lydia Whaley holding an herb medicine bottle around 1926. Moonshine was often the base substance and preservative for homemade medicines.

While some mountain churches embraced the temperance movement, most, even the Baptists and the Methodists, only discouraged drunkenness and promoted moderation. In the antebellum period, it was common for deacons and elders in Smokies churches to drink alcohol or even produce it. Indeed, the pastor of the church would not draw stares if he had a flask of whiskey on his hip.

Most social events in the mountains were accompanied by consumption of corn liquor, and while most folks drank in moderation, these events could lead to excessive guzzling. Occasions such as barn raisings, log rollings, hog killings, and corn huskings were times for male social drinking. Traveler Charles Lanman commented that by the time he arrived at a barn raising in Buncombe County, North Carolina in 1848, "an abundance of whiskey had already been imbibed." Militia musters and court days also prompted heavy drinking. Augustus Merrimon observed a court day in Burnsville, North Carolina where the crowd of Yancey Countians "tried to see how badly they could behave themselves. At different times I noticed groups about over the Court Yard and in the center stood a large gawky fellow with a fiddle and he would saw off some silly ditty. Two or three drunken fools would dance to the same."

Elections and election days also provoked a good many individuals to drink to excess in mountain communities. Voters generally expected those running for office to "treat" them with whiskey and provide some entertainment. Traveler Kemp Plummer Battle noted this style of "mountain canvassing" by a candidate for the North Carolina General Assembly in Burnsville in 1848: "The candidate, a man named Fleming, spoke from a goods-box in front of a grog-shop most animatedly and effectively, for about an hour with a tin quart-pot in his right hand. Then he went into the shop inviting the crowd to follow him to partake of whiskey. He was elected."

Aside from the cultural and social dimensions of alcohol consumption in the Smokies, corn liquor and brandy served as the base for many commonly used folk remedies. There was a strong belief that alcohol was "good for what ails you," whatever that may be. Augustus Merrimon observed that farmers in Western North Carolina generally believed "that to drink [whiskey] in damp and cold weather will warm them and to drink in hot weather it will cool them."

Whiskey was used in remedies for croup, dysentery, toothache, headache, colds, flu, and snakebite. One Swain County resident told Horace Kephart that while people in the Smokies generally relied on herbal cures because of the distance to doctors and their "scand'lous" costs, the herbs "customarily ain't no good 'thout a leetle grain o' whiskey." According to the students at Rabun Gap Nacoochee School in Dillard, Georgia who collected mountain remedies for the *Foxfire* series of books, the best treatment for snakebite was to "cut open a freshly killed chicken and place its guts onto the bite to draw poison. Drink whiskey, and also apply it to the bite." The cure for colds and flu called for a double dose of corn liquor: "Whiskey and honey and lamb's tongue and whiskey." According to Reed Stanley of North Georgia, brandy also had wonderful medicinal qualities. "Any of these doctors will tell you that brandy and honey is the healthiest things to lungs they've ever seen. It's the best cough syrup ever made."

In addition to its social and medicinal uses, perhaps the most significant aspect of the production of corn liquor in the Smokies prior to the Civil War was its economic importance. While many look back at the folks in the region as living a pioneer, self-sufficient existence, recent research—led by historian Durwood Dunn in his book *Cades Cove: The Life and Death of a Southern Appalachian Community, 1818-1937*—has revealed that Smokies residents were tied into market relationships with local towns, plantations to the east and south, the growing American cities, and even international markets as far away as China. Even relatively self-sufficient farmers needed something to trade for goods they could not produce themselves such as iron goods, coffee, or salt. Land-owning farmers also needed at least some cash money in order to pay their property taxes as the tax-man would not accept a hog or bushels of corn as in-kind payment. As Joseph Dabney observed, "What the

Although famers grew many crops in the Smokies, including wheat, oats, rye, and myriad vegetables, corn was the staple for food and commerce.

settler needed was a cash crop to enable him to pay his taxes and thus retain his precious property—usually a few hundred acres." Even non-land owning tenants needed some way to pay their rents.

Farmers in the Smokies basically had two major products that they could produce that had real cash value and were easily transportable—livestock and whiskey. Many used both avenues to purchase market goods and pay their taxes. Turning their corn crop into whiskey, even if they relied on a more skilled community distiller, provided one of the most profitable uses of the farmers' time and resources. As W. J. Rorabaugh observed, "A farmer could realize handsome profits from processing his grain into spirits, since a bushel of corn worth 25 cents yielded 2 ½ gallons of spirits worth $1.25 or more. Even if the farmer did not do his own distilling and had to give a commercial distiller half the output in payment for his services, he could increase the value of his corn by 150 percent." In a region where transportation of goods was at best difficult, the portability of whiskey made it an ideal trade product. "A horse could carry about $2 worth of corn," Dabney noted, "but $16 worth of corn liquor." Demand for corn liquor was also strong as it displaced rum as the favored spirit in the United States in the early years of the 19th century. Westward expansion away from the coasts, the repeal of the whiskey excise tax during Thomas Jefferson's administration, and tariffs imposed on molasses and rum imported from the Caribbean made the local product more attractive.

In addition, whiskey production provided other economic benefits to Smokies residents. Barrel makers, blacksmiths, metal workers, and potters found ready markets for stills, still parts, and containers. Skilled distillers were also in high demand and commanded top wages in the region. A Jonesboro, Tennessee newspaper ran an ad in 1825 for such a position: "Wanted immediately, a first rate distiller. A young man without family, who understands the art of distilling corn and rye mixed, and all rye. He must be a man of sober habits. To such a one constant employment and good wages will be given."

Many distillers also supplemented their income by feeding still slops to hogs, their most marketable product. Hogs love corn mash and as the authors of the *Foxfire* series noted, whiskey producers in the mountains, "were forced to put fences around their stills to keep hogs, who were kept on 'open range' then, from falling into the mash boxes and drowning." Historian Wilbur Miller argued that for many small distillers, "there was actually more profit in the hogs than in the whiskey." While serving in the U.S. House of Representatives, future President James Buchanan asserted that many "distillers' profits depended less upon whiskey than upon hogs fattened on distilling slop." Even in the modern-day Great Smoky Mountains National Park, wildlife technicians sometimes use corn mash to bait an especially trap-shy wild hog.

It is difficult to judge the exact amount of corn whiskey and brandy produced in the Smokies during the antebellum period as most small distillers did not keep account books and their small operations did not appear in official records. The available reports indicate that whiskey making, common everywhere during the antebellum period, was more prevalent in the mountain regions than in other parts of the country. While Western North Carolina held only 14% of the population of the state in 1840, it produced 31% of the state's whiskey. It should be noted that this did not include the thousands of small, seasonal distillers in the mountains who made whiskey for home consumption or for local markets.

Records of the whiskey market do appear in the account books and ledgers of some of the larger store owners in the region. These documents indicate that liquor was one of the most frequently purchased items and that it was even more commonly used by patrons to purchase other store goods. Indeed, the "pint of whiskey" was one measure of currency and even had a standard equivalent of 3.5 grains of gold. One of the leading store owners from 1792 to 1830 in Western North Carolina was John Carson of McDowell County. After reviewing Carson's account books, John Parris reported in the *Asheville Citizen-Times* in 1982, that the "single item occurring with the most frequency is whiskey or some other form of distilled liquor." The ledgers of William Holland Thomas, a prominent Western North Carolina store owner in Jackson and Cherokee Counties from 1822 to the 1870s, also show a sizeable trade in liquor, despite the fact that Thomas joined his adopted father Yonaguska in a campaign to promote temperance among the Qualla Cherokee.

In the words of Joseph Dabney, for farmers in the Smokies, the era from earliest white settlement up to the Civil War constituted a "golden era of American whiskey as a tax-free agricultural enterprise and frontier cottage industry." For elites, land-owning yeoman farmers, and even tenants in the Great Smoky Mountains, making and drinking whiskey were tremendously important. "Before the Civil War, no stigma had yet been attached to mountain residents who made alcohol," observed historian Bruce Stewart. Antebellum distillers "were therefore not marginalized criminals but entrepreneurs responding to the marketplace. As such, they gained the appreciation of mountain people, who regarded drinking—and distilling—as a vital element of their economy and culture."

CHAPTER 2
THE TAX MAN COMETH

The beginning of the end for this "golden era" for whiskey distillers in the Great Smoky Mountains came in 1862 when the U.S. Congress enacted an excise tax on whiskey. The initial tax was 20 cents per gallon, but by the end of the Civil War had been increased to $2 per gallon. Of course, that first legislation had little effect on distillers in the mountain South, as both Tennessee and North Carolina were part of the Confederacy and folks had other things on their mind. Indeed, enforcement of the excise tax in the Smokies was in a state of benign neglect until around 1876 when federal revenue agents focused their attention on bringing the large legally registered distilleries across the nation into compliance with the law. In addition, federal authorities feared igniting new hostilities against the Union during the Reconstruction period.

The excise tax on whiskey was not something new in American history, or for that matter in the history of the English, Scots, and Irish ancestors of most Smoky Mountain distillers. The English first imposed a tax on whiskey in Scotland and Ireland in 1644 and met immediate resistance. Scottish poet Robert Burns even put his condemnation of the "gaugers" who enforced the law in exclamation-laden verse:

> Thae curst horse-leeches o' the Excise
> Wha mak the whiskey stills their prize!
> Hand up thy han', Deil! Ance, twice, thrice!
> There, seize the blinkers!

An bake them up in brunstane pies
For poor damn'd drinkers.

Even killing gaugers in some precincts was not seen as going
too far. One Irish historian has noted, "Wherever it could be done
with comparative safety, he [the gauger] was hunted to the death."
Making illicit whiskey and smuggling it to market became huge growth
industries throughout the British Isles and the notion that making
whiskey was a basic human right an integral part of Celtic culture.

In the United States, one of Alexander Hamilton's worst ideas was
imposition of an excise tax on whiskey in 1791. Famously, inhabitants
of western Pennsylvania launched the Whiskey Rebellion in response
and President Washington had to retrieve his general's uniform out of
mothballs in 1794 and ride out at the head of 15,000 militiamen and
re-establish U.S. authority in the region. Truth be told, the conscious
effort made by the federal government not to enforce the law very
strictly after the unpleasantness in Pennsylvania contained widespread
rebellion throughout the American backcountry. Congress repealed
the tax altogether in 1800, when a Democratic-Republican majority
gained control of the legislative branch under the leadership of Thomas
Jefferson. Indeed, opposition to the whiskey excise aided Jefferson and
the Republicans in their victory over John Adams and the Federalists.
Legislators enacted an excise tax once again during the War of 1812
as part of a general commodities tax, but did not strictly enforce it.
Although the tax aroused little opposition, Congress repealed it in 1817.

The excise tax of 1862 did not draw universal condemnation in the
Great Smokies region; and a number of the larger operations registered
with the government, once enforcement began and the tax was dropped
to 50 cents per gallon in 1868. George Powell and Jules Gregg operated
a large legal distillery in the Chestnut Flats area near Cades Cove that
produced both corn liquor and brandy. Powell had some of the largest
peach and apple orchards in the area. There was also a legal distillery in
Cataloochee on the Boaz Whaley place that produced liquor for several

years. The Cosby section of Cocke County had a "government still" between Mill Creek and Indian Creek that produced sizeable amounts of whiskey up until county-wide prohibition took effect in 1906. While records are sketchy, and most evidence is anecdotal, it appears that the Smokies harbored numerous legal, tax-paying liquor operations during this period, although their numbers ebbed and flowed with increases and cuts in the excise tax and the rise of local and statewide temperance and prohibition movements.

For most Smoky Mountains distillers, particularly farmers who used whiskey to supplement their income and for home and neighborhood consumption, paying the excise tax was out of the question and would have reduced their already meager profits. Farmers still needed cash to pay property taxes and purchase store items; and

Author and scholar Horace Kephart (right) came to the Smokies in 1904 and wrote widely about mountain folk. He was especially interested in moonshiners and their cat-and-mouse relationship with the law.

transportation problems and the lingering after effects of the Civil War limited available options for raising the needed funds. As one Swain County, North Carolina neighbor told Horace Kephart, "Corn juice is about all we can tote around over the country and git cash money for. Why, man, that's the only way some folks has o' paying their taxes." The only choice for many was to go underground and start making whiskey illegally. Indeed, if anything, production of whiskey went up in the Smokies with the enactment of the excise tax as the rugged terrain provided an excellent place to hide a still. In addition, the liquor tax made the legal product more expensive to consumers and thus the illegal one even more profitable.

The small farmers of the Smokies were an independent lot, and many bristled at the notion that the federal government would attempt to deprive them of what they saw as one of their basic rights. The Civil War of course still loomed large in the minds of many residents of the Smokies. Those who had sided with the Confederacy saw the excise tax as another example of Yankee meddling. The many Unionists in the mountains chafed at the fact that a government they had fought to save was now making it more difficult for them to make a living. For both sides, it was a matter of government interfering with their independence. The so-called Poet Laureate of the Smokies, Ella V. Costner, characterized this attitude eloquently as she recalled her early days in Cosby, Tennessee: "We were taught independence of every phase of society, independence of all fads of fashion, independence of caste or convention, or creed, or color, independence from all forms of Government and Law, save what was right in the sight of God. Thus did my father live. No laws nor reforms of whatever moment could affect him. He was king of his domain, no matter how humble."

While the basic process of making whiskey did not change, several important aspects of the business did. First of all, the once honorable occupation of producing un-taxed whiskey was now illegal—at least in the eyes of the federal government—and the distiller became an outlaw. Along with this outlaw status, terminology for the distiller changed as well. In popular parlance—particularly in the press—the maker became a "moonshiner" and his product "moonshine." In the Smokies, however, the illegal distillers referred to themselves more often as "blockaders" and the product "blockade liquor." As Horace Kephart wrote, by way of explanation, illegal distillers used the term blockader, "thereby proclaiming that they risked and fought for a principle, so the moonshiner considers himself simply a blockade runner dealing in contraband." Of course, in the South the term blockader or blockade runner had romantic and positive connotations from the Civil War. The term bootlegger also came into common usage for one who sells illegal alcohol, not necessarily the maker.

More importantly than mere changes in terminology, however, distillers-turned-outlaw-moonshiners/blockaders had to change their behavior in significant ways. Producers now had to go to great lengths to conceal their operations. Proximity to good water was still crucial to the whiskey-making process, but now the illegal distillers generally had to locate their stills far up in mountain hollows. Blockaders prized locations that were both difficult for revenue agents to access and provided ready escape routes. Horace Kephart vividly described the typical illegal still location in the Smokies and the lengths moonshiners went to make sure they did not leave any sign of their activities: "Some little side-branch is chosen that runs through a gully choked with laurel and briers and rhododendron as to be quite impassable, save by such worming and crawling as must make a great noise. Doubtless a faint cattle-trail follows the backbone of the ridge above it, and this is the workers' ordinary highway in going to and fro; but the descent from ridge to gully is seldom made twice over the same course, lest a trail be printed direct to the still-house."

Blockaders also had to screen their operations from revenue agents, informers, or innocent wayfarers. They often felled a large tree, particularly an evergreen such as a hemlock, on the down-hill side of his still. The branches of the tree would also help disperse the smoke from the fire to help avoid detection. They also might move operations to the base of a cliff, or even into a cave, to secure at least one side. Many moonshiners built a small shed, or still house, over their stills to help conceal them and to protect them from the elements.

Now that their business was illegal, blockaders had to be much more choosy about the type of fuel they used to stoke their furnaces. Of course hardwoods had always been favored as they produced hotter and steadier fires. Now illegal distillers had to be concerned about which woods produced the least smoke to make sure the stills did not attract the attention of revenue agents. When they could get it, moonshiners preferred either locust or green ash. As one moonshiner told Joseph Dabney, he preferred green ash as it "just lays there and fries, and don't make no racket or no smoke." Of course, locust and green ash were not always readily available, so the moonshiners had to use the hardest wood they could find at hand.

Another problem for the moonshiner was where and how to obtain corn malt. Along with the excise tax, authorities also required millers to be licensed to grind malt to control the supply. Many blockaders got around this by using small tub mills, common on mountain farms, although their slow pace of grinding limited their output. At other times, moonshiners conspired with owners of grist mills to illegally grind malt on the sly or even broke into the mills at night to grind it. Raymond Caldwell recalled this happening at his father's grist mill in Cataloochee. "They'd slip in at night-time and grind it under the nose of my father." The next morning, Caldwell would discover the malt residue which caused him more work as "you'd have to re-bed your rockers to get rid of that so you wouldn't have that fermented stuff."

The excise tax and the rise of blockading also led to the end, for most whiskey makers, of aging their product. Moonshiners had to be mobile and ready to take their still and run if they sensed the presence of revenue agents. As Horace Kephart observed, "He has enough to conceal, or run away with, a mere copper still, to say nothing of barrels of whiskey." In addition, most blockaders were relatively poor and needed their money quickly, even if it was only to purchase more stills or materials for making whiskey. As a practical matter, illegal distillers got their whiskey out quickly to market. Kephart shared a common story in *Our Southern Highlanders* on legendary Smokies moonshiner Aquilla "Quill" Rose's views on the merits of aging whiskey: "A slick-faced dude from Knoxville told me once that all good red-liquor was aged, and that if I'd age my blockade it would bring a

Legendary moonshiner Quill Rose stands on his front porch with a scythe. He lived along Eagle Creek and was often celebrated in the popular press of the late 19th and early 20th centuries.

fancy price. I kept some for three months—and, by godlings, it ain't so."

Making moonshine was a strenuous business and the stereotype of the "lazy moonshiner" is a long way from the reality of the actual work involved. As still sites generally lay far off the "beaten path," blockaders had to carry stills, "rawhide" in sacks of cornmeal and malt, and then haul the product out, all through heavy brush and up and down steep mountainsides. Arthur Young, who made illegal liquor in the shadow of Clingmans Dome as a young man recalled the work: "I've heard said back in them days, 'That man ought to be out workin' instead of makin' likker, He ain't doin' nothing, just taking it easy.' The fact was, the moonshiners were the ones who were really working. We carried meal on our backs . . . . A bushel of meal would weigh 62 pounds . . . . I was stout. At 18, I didn't know how stout I was. We brought liquor out in five and ten-gallon kegs." This was on top of the normal heavy labor and intensity inherent in making whiskey. All the while, blockaders had to be on high alert for spies or revenue agents, never knowing when they would have to make a run for it through the laurel to maintain their freedom. As one moonshiner put it, "Blockadin' is the hardest work a man ever done. And hit's wearin' on a feller's narves."

The vast majority of Smokies residents in the blockade business were small, seasonal producers, working with other family members as they did on the farm. Family members not only provided cheaper labor, but also were much less likely to inform authorities. Making moonshine was small farmers' hedge against hard times, and by keeping their operations small, sporadic, and well hidden, they could generally escape the attention of federal revenue agents.

The Smokies did produce, and harbor, more than their fair share of large-scale, illegal operations, and even some individuals characterized in the press as "moonshine kings." Although introduced primarily as a legendary deer and bear hunter, Quill Rose's reputation as a blockader became national when Wilbur Zeigler and Ben Grosscup's 1883 book, *The Heart of the Alleghanies*, featured him. Rose had a fairly sizeable operation on Eagle Creek on the western edge of the Smokies throughout the late 19th century and hauled whiskey as far away as Knoxville. He became even more famous later in life when Horace Kephart expanded on his legend 30 years later.

On the other side of Gregory Bald in Chestnut Flats, George Powell and Jules Gregg, tired of paying the excise tax, turned their legal distillery into a "wildcat" blockade operation in the 1870s. The two had a sizeable business and regularly hauled wagon loads of whiskey and brandy to Maryville hidden under pumpkins or other produce. In 1878 the *Maryville Index* reported that deputy revenue agent Elias Cooper had raided Powell's "isolated rum mill" and destroyed eleven tubs of beer, four tubs of fruit pomace, 130 gallons of brandy singlings, five bushels of meal, two bushels of rye, and two bushels of malt. Although Powell, "the engineer of the mash mill," was arrested, he "subsequently escaped while the men and women of the household were abusing and threatening the officers."

In the late 1870s and early 1880s, Hut Amarine, also of Blount County, became known by many revenue agents as "chief of the Smoky mountain operators" and "one of the most daring outlaws in the Union." In 1878, Amarine killed Elias Cooper's son John during a raid. Agents arrested the moonshiner twice and "both times [he] broke jail, and made good his escape." Amarine's gang "established such a reign of terror" in Blount County that officials and civilians alike were "literally afraid to do or say anything against them." Authorities finally arrested him in 1881.

While the most famous moonshiner in the entire southern Appalachian region did not start out in the Smokies, Lewis Redmond ended his career as a blockader in Swain County, in a hollow outside Bryson City. Redmond commenced his career in the illegal liquor business in southwest North Carolina in what is now Transylvania County. In 1876, he shot and killed federal marshal Alfred Duckworth, who had stopped Redmond as he transported a load of untaxed corn liquor to market. After the shooting, Redmond fled to the so-called "Dark Corners" of Greenville, Pickens, and Oconee County, South Carolina. There he established an extensive illegal distilling operation and formed a criminal gang that terrorized federal officials. Redmond became a favorite of Democratic Party politicians in that state, including Governor Wade Hampton, as an exemplar of defiance of "Yankee oppression." Profiled in lengthy articles in the *Charleston News and*

Courier, the *New York Times*, and the *National Police Gazette*; Redmond
also became the subject of two fanciful dime novels widely circulated
nationally and even in Europe, one that gave him the title "King of the
Moonshiners."

Redmond's fame came with a cost, however, and by 1879 the
pressure from determined federal agents forced him to flee to the
Great Smoky Mountains of Swain County, North Carolina. There
he continued his moonshining activities, although not on as large a
scale. On April 7, 1881 federal marshals finally captured Redmond
at his home near Charleston (now Bryson City) after a shoot-out that
left him with six bullet wounds. Prosecutors decided not to indict
him for the murder of Duckworth; in exchange he pled guilty to eight
violations of federal revenue law and two counts of criminal conspiracy
and was sentenced to ten years in the federal penitentiary in Auburn,
New York. After Redmond served three years in prison, President
Chester A. Arthur pardoned him at the request of (now) Senator
Wade Hampton. Subsequently Redmond made a triumphal return to
Upstate South Carolina. Distiller Dietrich Biemann hired the "King
of the Moonshiners" to run his legal operation in Oconee County and
Redmond's picture even graced the bottle of one of Biemann's most
popular products. Sensational and exaggerated local and national press
reports on the exploits of Redmond, Quill Rose, Hut Amarine, and the
denizens of Chestnut Flats, and the fact that national journalists often
inaccurately used the term "Smoky Mountains" for the entire southern
Appalachian region, helped make the area synonymous with the large-
scale production of illegal liquor and defiance of federal authority.

A big part of the reason for this widespread press coverage in the
late 1870s and early 1880s was a crackdown by the Bureau of Internal
Revenue that specifically targeted the mountain South, including
the Great Smoky Mountains. In 1877, the new Commissioner of the
Bureau, Green B. Raum, a former brigadier general in the Union Army,
declared war on the moonshiners and their defiance of federal law. In
his bi-annual report for 1876-77, Raum asserted that in "the past year

not less than 3,000 illicit stills have been operated" in the mountain regions of Virginia, Kentucky, Tennessee, North Carolina, Alabama, and Georgia. With each of those stills producing ten to fifty gallons of illegal liquor a day, running at least twenty days per month, four months of the year, he estimated the government lost $2.5 million in revenue annually. In addition, this "open and notorious" defiance of federal authority demanded that "extraordinary measures be required to break them up." Raum received additional funding from Congress so that revenue agents could hire from five to ten deputies to aid them; he charged U.S. marshals to cooperate with agents to apprehend violators, and encouraged federal district attorneys to "prosecute all offenders."

Revenue collectors fanned out across the Smokies to track down stills and apprehend violators. They looked for signs of well-used trails into mountain hollows, wisps of smoke that would indicate still fires, and, like the moonshiners themselves, looked for plants that indicated soft water and followed streams up into coves to look for stills. They even tracked the feral hogs they knew were attracted to mash and still slops. One revenue agent in the Smokies used his horse's distaste for slop-tainted water in tracking down illegal operations. His horse had the habit of taking a drink in every stream he crossed. If the horse tasted even a little still slop in the water, he refused to drink and tossed his head. The agent then took his horse upstream where he often found a still.

The most effective, and controversial, tactic, however, to find illegal operations was to hire informants. People in the Smokies informed on their neighbors for a number of reasons. Some sought revenge over family feuds, business deals gone bad, or for notifying authorities of their illegal activities. Indeed, one tactic commonly used by revenue agents when they arrested someone was to imply that some neighbor, who they also suspected of blockading, had turned them in. Sometimes a wife or mother reported their own husband or son, especially if they were chronically drunk and/or abusive. Whatever the reason, informants proved both effective and universally despised in the Smokies. As one moonshiner told the students collecting oral histories for the *Foxfire* project, "Th' lowest man I know is one who wins your confidence, buys your liquor, and then turns you in. I believe there's a special place for people like that after they die." Indeed, fear of informants did make many Smokies residents suspicious of outsiders and led to tensions in mountain communities, violence against those suspected of notifying authorities, and even revenge killings. One newspaper reporter in the region argued that enforcing the revenue law with "a lot of spies and smellers" was "repulsive to a free people."

Revenue agents tried to catch blockaders in the act, but even if they did not, they generally destroyed the still, dumped out mash and beer, and poured out, or confiscated, any whiskey or brandy on hand. Although they usually just took an axe to the still, Western North Carolina agents developed a special tool called a "devil" that had a hatchet blade on one end and a pointed pick on the other. They used the pick end to poke holes in the copper sheeting until, as Horace Kephart described it, the still "looked somewhat like a gigantic horseradish-grater

Women and children sometimes served as lookouts at stills. They would sound the alarm by yelling or firing a gun when any strangers were sighted in the vicinity.

turned inside out." Such treatment rendered a still virtually irreparable. Agents would also take a stick and straighten the worm. Kephart described one deputy who "triumphantly carried away with him the copper-sheathed staff, as legal proof, trophy, and burgeon of office."

While the initial crackdown by the Bureau of Internal Revenue in the late 1870s produced a number of arrests and the destruction of hundreds of stills, it created widespread popular resistance, a violent backlash, political opposition, and actually galvanized communities in the Smokies and the rest of the mountain South in opposition to federal law enforcement. Smoky Mountain moonshiners did not sit idly and let the federal government destroy their livelihood.

Communities developed warning systems that alerted blockaders of the first signs of revenue agents. Moonshiners trained their children to warn adults of the presence of an outsider and mountain women stayed on the alert when their men were at the still. If someone spotted a suspicious person, they fired warning shots in the air or sounded a hunting horn and soon the hollows and hills echoed as the alarm spread. As Joseph Dabney put it, "after one blast, another would answer in the next cove, and soon the whole region would resound like Gideon's Army on the march." As soon as they heard the sound, blockaders broke down their stills and took everything—especially pot, cap, and coil—into hiding. East Tennesseee Revenue Collector Joseph Spurrier declared that "the moonshiners found out I was in the mountains before I full knew the fact myself . . . . In an hour after the first [horn] blast people one hundred miles away knew that Spurrier was on a raid. I didn't get a dog's chance to seize a still."

If apprehended, the tendency of most blockaders, particularly the so-called "little moonshiners," was to come along quietly and not resort to violence. The key to avoid getting shot, as one moonshiner put it, was to avoid having a gun on you. In addition, the relatively small investment they had in their operations, the relatively light penalties—at most a year and a day in a federal penitentiary—and the real likelihood that a local judge or jury might acquit you made blockaders take a philosophical attitude toward arrest and even incarceration. Moonshining was a game of cat-and-mouse, and as long as both sides played by the rules of that game—you've got to physically catch a man in the act, you don't shoot at people who don't shoot at you, treat your prisoners with respect, do not get mad or violent if they "cut down" your still, they are only doing their job—then no one got hurt and revenuers and moonshiners could mutually respect one another and even be friends. As one neighbor told Horace Kephart, "Hit's as fair for one as 'tis for t'other. When a revenuer comes sneakin' around, why whut he gits, or whut we-uns gits, that's a 'fortune of war,' as the old sayin' is."

In the late 1870s and early 1880s, however, particularly with the "big moonshiners," the campaign to enforce the revenue laws began to take on the character of a real war, with real casualties. The likes of Lewis Redmond and Hut Amarine had too much at stake with large capital investments and warrants for their arrest for charges much more serious than simple revenue law violations, including capital murder. They were not going to go along quietly and take their chances in court, and their heavily armed gangs were not either, as the stories of Redmond and Amarine reveal. In 1898, when agents raided George Powell's still in Chestnut Flats and destroyed it, friends and family ambushed revenue agents on their way back to Maryville and as the *Maryville Index* reported, "a lively fusillade ensued." No one was wounded or killed, but the exchange of gunfire put an exclamation point on the seriousness of the situation and significantly upped the stakes for both sides in this war.

While the hills and hollows of the Smokies echoed with the sound of hunting horns and gunfire, the "Moonshine Wars" prompted an intense political debate in the region. In Western North Carolina, the Democratic Party tried to regain ground lost during the Reconstruction Era and characterized revenue enforcement as a Republican Party plot to deny law-abiding citizens of their inalienable rights. As former vice president of the Confederacy Alexander Stephens put it, "a farmer should have the same right to boil his corn into 'sweet mash' as to boil it into hominy." In 1876 on the campaign trail for a third term as Governor of North Carolina, Buncombe County native Zebulon B. Vance vehemently asserted—as he held up a jar with a grasshopper preserved in alcohol—that federal revenue agents were a blight on the landscape akin to "red-legged grasshoppers. This fellow," he continued, "eats up every green thing that God ever gave to man, and he only seeks universal dissolution! The time has come when an honest man can't take an honest drink without a gang of revenue officers after him."

While other issues played a role in the Democratic Party resurgence in Western North Carolina—especially opposition to civil and voting rights for African-Americans—the revenue enforcement issue proved to be an effective one and helped the Democrats make significant political gains in the late 1870s. Counties that had been dependably Republican in the late 1860s, were solidly in the Democratic Party camp by 1876. Henderson County Republican Hamilton Ewart bemoaned the "odium which existed against the Internal Revenue law, and the hatred and contempt entertained by the people for its execution." He placed the blame for his party's losses squarely at the feet of Democrats effective at "saddling the responsibility of its passage [the revenue law] upon the Republican Party."

The Moonshine Wars also had important political repercussions in the solidly Republican East Tennessee Smokies. Mountain Republicans regularly complained that denying them their rights and privileges to supplement their income by making un-taxed whiskey was a slap in the face as they had been "entirely loyal" to the Union during the Civil War. This vocal opposition helped influence important changes in revenue enforcement by the early 1880s.

By 1878, commissioner Green Raum realized that while his revenue collectors won many battles, they were losing the war in the Smokies. He called for a change in tactics and teamed up with the likes of federal judge Robert Dick and head collector in the Sixth Collection District of Western North Carolina, J. J. Mott, to find ways to gain greater acceptance of the Bureau of Internal Revenue and promote the legal liquor industry in the area. The first thing they did was to clean house and get rid of corrupt agents. The BIR had gained a bad reputation nationally due to the Whiskey Ring scandal that almost unseated the Grant administration in 1875. On the local and regional level, critics characterized the Bureau as a haven for unqualified and corrupt political appointees where the only prerequisite for a job was loyalty to the Republican Party. Raum remained a staunch defender of political patronage, and publicly declared

"Leslie's Weekly" was a popular news and literary magazine that was published from 1852 to 1922. It was renowned for its wood engravings like this one showing "an illicit whiskey-still in the mountains being surprised by revenue officers." The issue is September 1, 1883.

that he would "not appoint a Democrat if I knew it," but he encouraged District Collectors like Mott to fire deputies who drank excessively or were unnecessarily violent, raised the qualifications for deputy collectors, and determined to "hire men of character and honesty."

While hiring collectors with better character helped, the changes made in official policy made the most difference. First, Raum instituted a guiding principle of "selective leniency" that offered first time offenders suspended sentences if they agreed to end their illegal activities. Next, the Bureau reduced the capacity for government-registered, tax-paying stills from six to three and one-half bushels of corn to allow more small producers to qualify. In the Sixth District, legal stills increased from 42 in 1878 to 198 in 1879 and Collector Mott claimed in a letter to Raum, "the old moonshiners are nearly all at work under the law and those who are not intimidated and kept out by those who are." By 1882, Raum asserted that the Sixth District had been "lifted up from the attitude of fraud and resistance to authority into an observance of the law." Federal revenue collectors could now crisscross the district "without being bushwacked, whereas, five years ago, a private citizen passing through that country with 'store' clothes on, and who was unknown to the people, was in danger of being suspected as a revenue officer and shot." By the mid-1880s, the open rebellion in the Smokies had died down although illegal distilling remained relatively common, particularly among small producers in the more isolated parts of the region.

National press coverage of the "Moonshine Wars" and the exploits of colorful and violent blockaders like Hut Amarine and Lewis Redmond did leave a lasting legacy, however, in the rise of the "local color" literary movement where, in the words of historian Bruce Stewart, moonshining "became synonymous with the mountain region." In the late 19th century the writers in the movement provided colorful, and overly exaggerated, accounts of mountain living which helped create and popularize stereotypes of Appalachian people for the growing number of popular magazines like *Harper's*, *Appleton's*, *Lippincott's*, and the *Atlantic Monthly*. Many of the articles, and later books, were either directly about blockading—titles included, "Moonshiners," "The Moonshine Man," "Law and Moonshiners," "Among the Moonshiners," and "Home of the Moonshiners"—or featured moonshining as a key component of mountain life. As Stewart added, "During those years, illicit distilling became virtually a requirement in descriptive pieces dealing with the mountain region."

One of the most prolific and influential of the local color writers was Mary Noailles Murfree from Murfreesboro, Tennessee, who burst onto the national scene in the 1880s. Murfree spent considerable time at the Montvale Springs resort on the edge of the Smokies and took numerous horseback trips into Cades Cove and other areas of the western end of the range. Murfree, whose earlier work was published under the pseudonym of Charles Egbert Craddock, featured impoverished, ignorant, lazy, drunken, and generally violent moonshiners in many of her classic stories such as "Star in the Valley" and "The Moonshiners of Hoho-Hebee Falls." In "Star in the Valley," Murfree describes a gathering at a typical mountain home where "various family members of the family were seated on sundry domestic articles, such as wash-tubs, and splint-baskets made of white oak. There was circulating among Jerry Shaw's [the homeowner] friends a flat

The parts of a whiskey distillery (or still), from left to right, are the still pot, the thumper keg, and the worm.

bottle, facetiously denominated 'tickler,' readily emptied, but as readily replenished from a keg in the corner. Like the widow's cruse of oil, that keg was miraculously never empty. The fact of a still near by in the wild ravine might suggest a reason for its perennial flow."

Home missionaries and industrialists followed in the footsteps of local color writers and journalists covering the Moonshine Wars and used these stereotypical descriptions of the region, and its moonshiners, as concrete examples of the need for regional uplift either through "proper" churches, schools, railroads, industrial timber operations, coal mines, or textile mills. Even elites in the growing number of towns and cities in the Smokies region such as Asheville, Knoxville, Waynesville, Newport, and Maryville appropriated the stereotypes of the residents of nearby coves and hollows. As Stewart observed, "In their haste to differentiate themselves from mountain country folk, they identified their rural neighbors as a group of ignorant, drunk moonshiners."

The immediate post-Civil War era in the Great Smoky Mountains had been a traumatic one for residents, particularly for its whiskey makers. While Bureau of Internal Revenue Commissioner Green Raum could look back with pride on the success of the Moonshine Wars in the region, if he observed closely he could see that while the production of illegal alcohol had declined and the numbers of legal distilleries had increased by the late 1880s, moonshining had become an entrenched institution in the region. Indeed, it only took a little while for blockading to once again explode in the Smokies as changes that transformed the region in the 1890s and early years of the 20th century made what seemed to be a dying art more profitable and important than ever before.

CHAPTER 3

TEMPERANCE AND LACK THEREOF

The 1890s and beginning of the 20th century brought dramatic economic, political, social, and religious changes to the Smokies. Many observers heralded the dawn of the modern era, but others decried the ongoing presence of the moonshiner, a vestige of the region's past which served as a drag on regional progress. Most Smokies blockaders did not particularly care if they somehow hindered regional progress. Contrary to popular stereotypes, many moonshiners embraced modernity and sought to take advantage of new opportunities to lift themselves and their families out of poverty.

By the early 1890s, poverty was the watchword in the Smokies as many families faced ever worsening economic circumstances. In addition to federal authorities slamming the door on legal distilling, other traditional ways of supplementing farm income became less viable. The droving and selling of cattle and hogs declined as railroads pushed for closing of the open range to keep livestock off their tracks and also brought cheaper midwestern beef and pork into the region. Markets for medicinal herbs also faltered as valuable products like ginseng were over-harvested and others replaced with new manufactured medicines. Average farm size in the region shrank as birth rates remained inordinately high and residents continued to equally divide farms into ever smaller parcels among their heirs. These situations forced more and more farmers onto marginal land characterized by soils depleted of their fertility that quickly eroded. One farmer Horace Kephart talked with in the early 1900s declared he would only get two or three "severe craps"

39

[crops] out of a field he'd just cleared. When Kephart asked him if he would then rotate crops, the farmer replied, "La no! By that time the land will be so poor hit wouldn't raise a cuss fight."

A national economic depression in the early 1890s worsened conditions for farmers, as market prices fell off the cliff. More and more farmers faced the prospect of seeing their land, owned by their families for generations, auctioned off on the courthouse steps due to their inability to pay property taxes. Under such circumstances, making a little whiskey to help them hold on to their farms did not seem like such a bad thing.

In addition to widespread poverty, another factor that made blockading attractive to many enterprising residents of the Smokies was the increasing profits the business could bring. Three important changes made moonshining much more lucrative in the late 19th and early 20th centuries. First, the federal government, in need of additional revenue to cover a shortfall in tariff collections, increased the liquor tax from 90 cents per gallon to $1.10. This move in turn made legal distilling less profitable and illegal distilling more so. The tax increase turned many authorized producers into criminals and the potential profits lured Smokies farmers back into the blockade business or into it for the first time. According to historian Wilbur Miller, a farmer could get about $10 for a full wagon load of about 20 bushels of corn. If he converted that same corn into 60 gallons of whiskey he could net $75 at market. In addition, a wagon could hold 120 gallons of liquor so the farmer could make $150 per wagon load. With the new tax, a legal distiller could only make 50 cents of profit by distilling two bushels of corn, while the blockader could make $7.50 off the same amount.

A second change that boosted blockaders' potential profits and created a huge new market for the blockade liquor was the arrival of railroads and industry in the Smokies. By the late 1890s, new technologies allowed railroads to penetrate the deepest recesses and highest peaks of the region. Highly capitalized northern timber companies like the Little River Railroad and Lumber Company,

Industrial scale logging began to transform life in the Great Smoky Mountains in the late 1890s. One of the changes it brought was boosting the circulation of currency in the region and creating more local demand for the moonshiners' wares.

W. M. Ritter Lumber Company, and Champion Fibre Company began snapping up cheap, timber-rich land, laying railroad track into the mountains, and constructing huge mills with adjacent company towns like Townsend, Elkmont, Crestmont, Proctor, Forney, Smokemont, and Ravensford. Thousands of young men began pouring into these communities from the surrounding region, across the nation, and even from Europe to cut the timber.

These hard-working and hard-drinking men created a virtually captive market for Smokies moonshiners. Although company owners and foremen did everything they could to discourage the men from drinking "white mule," wily moonshiners found ways to relieve these men of their hard-won wages and provide them with cheap liquor. Quill Rose was

41

one of those who benefitted most from the arrival of the timber towns and camps, since he no longer had to transport his goods in buckboard wagons, over rough roads, and to distant markets as an even larger, even thirstier market had come to his Eagle Creek doorstep. In addition, Rose had a winning personality and—in the words of historian Clark Medford—was "such a sly and smooth operator" that he was able to slip a considerable amount of product past lumber company officials and local and federal law enforcement for several years until he was finally arrested, tried, and convicted in 1911 at the age of 74.

The arrival of textile mill towns on the edge of the Smokies also created a huge market for Smokies blockaders. Although mill towns tended to hire entire families, men working in the mills often sought a cheap and effective way to, at least temporarily, lift their spirits and dull their pain after long, hot days in the mills. Moonshine also helped provide workers with short vacations, as many headed for the woods for spells of binge drinking—or a "high-lonesome" in local parlance.

The third key change came, ironically, due to the explosive growth of the temperance and prohibition movements. As if there were not enough incentives for those with a talent for making whiskey to enter the moonshine market, the increasing challenges faced by legal distillers made blockading even more attractive and profitable. The rise of towns, growth of the middle class, the arrival of large industrial operations, and stronger and more centralized religious denominations helped spark an unstoppable movement to strictly control, and eventually ban, alcohol production altogether.

The campaign began to gain momentum in the towns and churches of the region in the late 1870s in the midst of the Moonshine Wars. In 1878, the editors of the *Webster Spectator* in Jackson County, North Carolina, called even the legal manufacture of whiskey "a curse on the county" and demanded, "Let it be put down." In nearby Waynesville in 1878, W. W. Stringfield argued that distillers—both legal and illegal—were "willing to endanger their own and their neighbors' souls and bodies to get a little 'hellfire' for 'campfire.'" He later asserted if liquor was banned, "our beautiful mountain country will 'blossom as the rose,' and our mothers, wives, sweethearts and sisters, will sing anthems of praise." Increasingly, Southern Baptists and Southern Methodists condemned any consumption of alcohol as a sin and even switched from wine to grape juice for communion, helping make the Welch family very wealthy. Many Baptist churches in the area during the period adopted a church covenant that called on members "to abstain from the sale and use of intoxicating drinks as a beverage." In 1892, the Tennessee Baptist Convention passed a resolution declaring, "The saloon is the enemy of all good, the friend of all evil."

The growth of industry in the region also provided powerful allies for small town elites and the Baptists and Methodists in the fight against alcohol. Mill owners and timber operators wanted sober and dependable employees with good work habits and often spoke out strongly against

The excesses and lawlessness that sometimes accompanied the moonshine enterprise attracted the scorn of the temperance movement that was near its zenith in the late 1800s. Churches in the Smokies were outspoken opponents to liquor consumption and the animosity continues to this day.

the evils of alcohol, even as they consumed it in their own homes, and banned its sale and consumption in their milltowns and timber camps. The experience of S. B. Tanner, owner of Henrietta Mills in Rutherford County, North Carolina, was fairly typical of owners and management in Smokies area mills: "When we built our mill villages, this vicinity was noted for its blockade distilleries, and we had no end of trouble among our operatives, which interfered seriously with the running of our mills, and it was difficult for us to retain decent and respectable people at our mills, on account of rowdyism, midnight brawls, etc."

To be sure the manufacture, and consumption, of illegal alcohol had its dark side in alcohol abuse and violence. Of course, the forces of propriety made sure to publicize any alcohol-related problems that cropped up in their communities. In Blount County, Tennessee local newspapers often featured the goings-on of the blockading Powells, Burchfields, and Roses in the Chestnut Flats community. In 1893, John Harvey Burchfield was shot dead by Theodore Rose in a drunken brawl. The *Maryville Times* reported that in the aftermath of the shooting, "A wife and three small children are left in destitute circumstances without any means of support." In 1897, Hale Hughes and Sam Burchfield ambushed and killed George Powell, Jr. (nephew of the original Chestnut Flats brandy king) for testifying against the two in a moonshine case. In 1901, another Sam Burchfield—better known as "Smoke"—shot and killed "Chicken Eater" John Tipton in an argument over politics at a party held in celebration of a "run-off" of blockade whiskey.

Residents of Cades Cove increasingly sought to distance themselves from the shenanigans and violence of Chestnut Flats. A 1904 article written by a Cades Cove resident in the *Maryville Record*, in an obvious jibe at the Chestnut Flats folks, asserted, "Some of our citizens seem to think that a medicine is no good unless it has whiskey in it. About a gallon to a spoonful of medicine." The first major history of Cades Cove written by A. Randolph Shields reflected the strong distaste expressed by many in the Cove for folks in the Flats, when he reported that the area was "periodically inundated by outlaws of all descriptions who drank, gambled, whored, and shot each other to pass the time."

Linguist Joseph Hall recorded an account of a "mean bunch" in the Cataloochee area headed up by a man he gave the pseudonym "Zeke" who burned "Creek George" Palmer's barn down and cut off the ears of a man named Miles. As Hall recounted, "'Zeke' felt he was justified in burning the barn because 'Creek George' Palmer was a good religious man and cut his still down. Similarly, the unfortunate Miles had his ears lopped off because he stole his partner's liquor in spite of 'Zeke's' having warned him about it repeatedly." As if to prove his "mean" *bona fides*, "Zeke" allegedly "carried the little dried up ears with him for many years as an amusement and a grim warning to others not to tamper with what was not their business."

Stories like these proved grist for the anti-alcohol forces mill and by the 1880s, their propaganda campaigns started to gain support among legislators. In North Carolina, the state legislature passed "local option" legislation in 1880 that prohibited alcohol near courthouses, churches, schools, and industrial establishments. To control sales of alcohol, and eliminate saloons in towns, lawmakers let communities set up government-controlled dispensaries which were the only places liquor could be sold; moreover no drinking on the premises was allowed. Waynesville became one of the first towns in the state with a dispensary in 1895 and Bryson City followed suit in 1899. In 1905, lawmakers banned the sale of "spirituous liquors" outside of incorporated towns with a population of over 1,000. Given the rural nature of the region, this effectively ended legal alcohol sales in much of Western North Carolina. The door finally slammed shut on legal alcohol production and sales altogether when a statewide prohibition referendum passed almost two-to-one in May 1908. As of January 1, 1909 North Carolina legally became a dry state.

Tennessee followed a similar path to prohibition. In 1877 and again in 1887, the legislature passed laws prohibiting the sale of alcohol within four miles of rural schools. Legislators extended the so-called

"Four-Mile Law" to include towns of fewer than 2,000 inhabitants in 1899 and fewer than 5,000 in 1903. The state further extended the four-mile ban in the larger municipalities and in 1907 Knoxville became totally dry. Local newspapers reported bells tolling and a parade which featured University of Tennessee students riding on a water wagon in celebration of the victory of the "dry" forces. After 1907, the only places one could legally buy alcohol in East Tennessee were Chattanooga and LaFollette.

By 1908, a prohibition majority controlled the state legislature and in 1910 staunch Baptist Ben Hooper—ironically from Cocke County, a place fast becoming one of the "Moonshine Capitals of the World"—was elected governor on a prohibition platform. Hooper served two terms and pushed through the "Jug Bill" which banned the transportation of liquor within the state and the importation of more than one gallon from outside the state and the "Nuisance Bill" which allowed as few as ten citizens to file a petition to local courts to shutter "saloons and gambling houses." The final nail in legal alcohol's coffin in Tennessee came in 1917 when, ironically named, Governor Thomas C. Rye pushed through the "Bone-Dry Bill" which closed all legal loopholes to the manufacture or transportation of alcoholic beverages in the state.

One important group of prohibition advocates not mentioned so far celebrated these events as well. Blockaders often openly supported these bills as prohibition made their business even more profitable by forcing out legal competitors. It also drove many of the former legal distillers into the moonshiner ranks. A number of Cocke County's most prominent and successful moonshiners learned to make high quality whiskey in large volumes at a legal operation there. As moonshiner's daughter Jean Costner Schilling recalled, when authorities closed the business in 1904 through the "Four-Mile Law," "they saw no need to cease their livelihood, so they went undercover. Because of what they learned at the distillery they made very fine corn whiskey."

Obviously, local, statewide, and later national prohibition did not have the desired effect on the blockade liquor business in the Great

Smoky Mountains—that is unless you were a moonshiner. Indeed, Horace Kephart, who watched the process first-hand in the North Carolina Smokies, commented that moonshining had grown "by leaps and bounds since the mountain region went dry." A *New York Times* reporter facetiously commented on one Western North Carolina town which he characterized as "'dry,' so dry in fact that 100 gallons of blockade whiskey serves a small town of 150 inhabitants of all ages and both sexes for a week's consumption . . . and 50 gallons provide for the festivities of the Fourth of July. The prevailing thirst due to the 'dryness' of the town is amazing."

The general process of making corn liquor in the Smokies did not change appreciably with the coming of prohibition and the increased demand for illegal liquor in the early years of the 20th century, but there were some important innovations. Relatively poor farmers seeking to hold on to their broken-down farms who saw making liquor as both an economic necessity and their right as free citizens of the United States continued to produce the bulk of the region's moonshine. However, with profits so high, mountain residents with an entrepreneurial bent and a little capital bought the product of the "little moonshiners" and provided at least part of the supplies and equipment, the marketing, and the distribution of the product. Other "kingpins" rarely, if ever, went near a still and hired poor farmers to make and distribute the whiskey for them. These mountain "businessmen" also pioneered the construction and use of larger-capacity stills like those used in many legal operations. As Kephart observed, these so-called "big blockaders" made "unlicensed whiskey on a fairly large scale. He may have several stills, operating alternately in different places, so as to avert suspicion. In any case, the still is large and the output is quite profitable. The owner himself may not actively engage in the work, but may furnish the capital and hire confederates to do the distilling for him, so that personally he shuns the appearance of evil."

In addition to the aggregation of small stills and the increasing size of some blockade operations, local and state prohibition in the early

20th century led to at least one significant change in the whiskey-making process: the addition of the "thump keg." The thump keg, or "doubler," was a barrel or keg placed between the still and the condenser. Fresh beer and/or backings were poured into the thump keg and the alcohol vapor from the still ran by pipe to the bottom of the barrel where it bubbled up through the beer and out the top through another pipe and into the condenser. This process filtered out many of the impurities contained in a singlings run and boosted the proof of the alcohol. The thump keg saved the distiller a tremendous amount of time and effort because it eliminated the need for running the liquor through the still a second time and still produced a quality product. This innovation allowed blockaders to meet the increased demand for their product in the early 20th century and boosted profits further.

Rhododendron thickets or "hells" were favorite places to conceal a still. Fortunately for moonshiners this vegetation is often found near mountain streams.

Another change during the period was the attraction of increasing numbers of women to the illegal liquor business. Moonshining, or more commonly bootlegging the illegal product, often provided an economic safety net for women, particularly widows, in uncertain economic times. In his 1908 novel *Beyond the Bluegrass*, George Creswell Gill has a character explain why the "Widow Mosely" is in the moonshine business: "Old Joe Mosely died, you know last winter. He was purty o'nery, but that's no difference now. It's [making moonshine] the only way a wider and her two boys has to make a livin'." Growing up in the Smoky Mountains, Imogene Eaker recalled that the timber boomtown of Bushnell, North Carolina had a well-known woman moonshiner who lived between the school and the church. The school teacher made students stop in front of her house and sing hymns en route to revival meetings at the church. In Cosby, Lizzie Ogle Hooper was a community fixture well known for sitting in a rocking chair on her front porch and selling moonshine for twenty-five cents a shot in re-purposed glass snuff containers.

While the role of the widow moonshiner/bootlegger fit traditional gender stereotypes in the region, some used the opportunities provided by the illegal business to break out of their traditional "separate sphere." In a 1911 article entitled "Strange Stories of the Internal Revenue Service," Catherine Frances Cavanaugh reported, "Women moonshiners are not uncommon [in the southern Appalachian region]; and they fight with the combined energy of wild cat and rattlesnake when they are discovered."

By the early years of the 20th century, federal officials who once believed they had won the war against blockaders in the Smokies now had an even greater problem on their hands and few resources to combat it. On paper, revenue agents had additional allies in state and local law enforcement, ostensibly tasked with enforcing local and state prohibition laws. However, local officials generally proved weak partners and their enforcement of the laws spotty, at best; particularly since many of the local law enforcement were related to the blockaders. Furthermore, local sheriffs had to run for re-election and did not want to alienate rural voters.

The federal government responded with a new crackdown and began to pursue the moonshiners aggressively, adding new recruits, many of them former moonshiners themselves who sought the steadier pay of a "regular" job. The new agents also knew where the moonshiners likely hid their stills. Some of these men, according to Horace Kephart, were "desperados, men already stained with blood and reckless or ruthless about shedding more." One particularly aggressive former moonshiner-turned revenue agent was Hol Rose of Swain County. As Kephart described him, "Rose displayed more than usual activity in running down offenders. He would take more trouble, and run more risks, than the average county officer. Man-hunting, for him, was a sport: he thoroughly enjoyed it." Rose's risk-taking cost him dearly later when moonshiner Babe Burnett shot and killed him.

For the most part, however, relations between moonshiners and law enforcement retained the character of the earlier era. Each believed they had work to do and did not begrudge folks on the other side trying to do their job to the best of their abilities as long as they played by the unwritten rules. In most cases, if officers caught a moonshiner fair and square "in the act," the prisoner came along quietly without the added embarrassment of being handcuffed. Revenue agents and the more respected local law enforcement officials often served warrants for arrest and then allowed the accused blockader to stay at home trusting them to appear at the appointed time in court. Asked if one moonshiner showed up in such a case, revenue agent Charlie Beck, in an interview with Horace Kephart responded, "Sure, he showed up, punctual to the minute, and he made bond. Then he invited me to come and stay with him any time I'm down there. We're the best of friends." It was also not uncommon in the Smokies for judges to parole a farmer hauled in for moonshining so that they could go home, work their crops, and then return after the harvest to serve their sentence.

Moonshiners also generally did not mistreat innocent hunters or hikers who stumbled on still sites, despite the common stereotype of evil, sadistic moonshiners murdering such folks. Kephart asked one of his neighbors what would happen to him if he was out hunting and stumbled upon an operating still. The neighbor responded that the moonshiners would probably make him stir the mash and taste some of the liquor as that "would make you one o' them in the eyes of the law." When asked if the blockaders would then mistreat him, the neighbor replied incredulously, "Shucks! Why, man, whut could they gain by hurtin' you? At the wust, s'posin' they was convicted by your evidence, they'd only git a month or two in the pen. So why should they murder you and get hung for it? Hit's all 'tarnal foolishness, the notions some folks has!" Of course, Kephart did not advocate folks going out and looking for stills; mountain folks did not take kindly to people sticking their noses into other people's business. But he was injecting some reality into a situation that had taken on mythical proportions.

Despite the stereotypes being thrown around in the news media, popular culture, and by prohibition advocates, most blockaders in the early years of the 20th century were regular folks, trying as best they could to provide for their families. Even the people trying to arrest them, like Charlie Beck, called them the "nicest kind of people." Many were sober, honest, upstanding members of their communities and, far from being lazy and lacking ambition, had a strong entrepreneurial spirit and sought to move up the economic and social scale. These individuals rarely consumed their own product, and virtually never to excess, and lived by the code that "liquor's for selling, not for drinking." As Roy D. Brown of the Cosby section of Cocke County observed: "Most moonshiners were upstanding citizens of the community. Everyone knew what they did. They attended church; their word was their bond. For them, making a jar of whiskey was no different than making a jar of apple butter, and no less of a need."

While town Baptists and Methodists publicly railed against any form of alcohol and led their communities, counties, and states in the successful fight for prohibition, rural churches in the Smokies generally proved much more tolerant of moderate liquor drinking and especially of liquor making. As Jean Costner Schilling, the daughter of notorious Cosby moonshiner Ike Costner, recalled, "Both of my grandparents were ministers, yet my mother and daddy and their brothers and sisters all made moonshine." Dick Denton, also of Cosby, remembered "very distinctly, one night we were having prayer meeting in our house in the living room, and right outside, my Daddy was loading cases of whiskey onto a truck. The preachers up here didn't emphasize that it was a sin to drink." Dr. Robert Woody, who grew up in Cataloochee, recalled that his justice of the peace Uncle Jim Hannah "liked to refresh himself with it [moonshine] occasionally . . . . Except when he was recovering from a weekend binge, he was an eloquent Sunday School teacher."

Religious institutions not only tolerated whiskey in the Smokies, in some cases they actually benefitted from its production. Marvin "Popcorn" Sutton claimed that his grandfather used the proceeds from several runs of blockade liquor to help build the Hemphill Baptist Church near Maggie Valley, North Carolina. To be sure, Hemphill Baptist was not the only church in the Smokies supported by the tithes and offerings of moonshining parishioners.

While it is hard to generalize the doctrinal beliefs of a denomination that prided itself on congregational independence, Primitive Baptists—common in the Smokies—seemed particularly tolerant towards the moonshiners in their midst. Primitives have never stopped using wine in communion and as historian Charles Thompson put it, "Teetotal prohibition was never a stated Primitive Baptist goal." In addition, Primitives opposed such "inventions of man" and "delusions of Satan" as Sunday Schools, missionary societies, Bible societies, and, in the late 19th and early 20th centuries, para-church temperance and prohibition groups like the Woman's Christian Temperance Union and the Anti-Saloon League. One prominent Georgia Primitve Baptist writer characterized the government crackdown on small producers of blockade liquor as an "obvious attack on poor people." As Durwood Dunn, the foremost expert on Cades Cove, noted, the Primitive Baptists in that area, while decrying the activities and excesses of the residents of Chestnut Flats, tolerated moderate, surreptitious use of alcohol and moonshining as a way of supplementing farm income. "If a cove farmer drank only moderately and if his main source of income was not from moonshining, his weakness was grudgingly tolerated."

Despite the complex realities of the life of moonshiners in the Smokies, in the early years of the 20th century the producers of American popular culture depicted them in an increasingly simplistic and stereotypical manner. With the modern era came a new, more powerful media, the silent film, to reinforce the images first spread across the nation by the local color literary movement. Silent film producers loved to make movies about people in the southern Appalachian region. Between 1904 and 1929, the industry produced 476 movies about mountaineers and almost all of them featured moonshine and moonshiners. Historian Anthony Harkins has referred to this genre as "cookie-cutter feud and moonshine melodramas." Biograph, one of the "big three" production companies of the era, released the first movie of this type—*The Moonshiner*—in 1904. The thirteen-minute movie was so successful that four years later the company still touted it as "the most widely known and most popular film ever made." This movie, and its countless imitators, solidified the southern Appalachian moonshiner as a stock popular culture figure and helped imbed the image of ignorant, violent, and lazy mountain people deeply in the American psyche.

While his intent was to humanize mountain people, writer Horace Kephart unwittingly fed into the popular equation of the people of the Great Smoky Mountains and moonshining in his 1913 masterwork *Our Southern Highlanders*. Although Kephart purported to "give a true picture of life among the mountaineers," his interest in the more sensational and curious aspects of Smoky Mountains culture skewed that picture. Kephart had a fascination with moonshining— and evidently a taste for corn liquor as well—and of the twenty chapters in his book, he devoted six completely to the subject and others contain significant material related to blockading. As author and Hazel Creek native Duane Oliver observed, "This book angered many Hazel Creek people for they felt he had painted a picture of all of them as being lazy, destitute and ignorant. He was not interested in the ordinary people of Hazel Creek but the more picturesque inhabitants such as bootleggers, moonshiners and bear hunters as well as those living in extreme poverty."

Town and city dwellers, who knew little of the social and economic challenges faced by their rural cousins, also embraced these stereotypes. Certain sections of the Smokies were tagged as havens for moonshiners and looked down on by others across the county or across state lines. Cosby moonshiner's son Dick Denton recalled his upbringing in Cocke County: "Time has helped me realize whiskey making was not really a bad thing . . . But, at the time, I was ashamed of it. I was ashamed of my parents being involved in it, and many times I wished that they were just average people who did average things for a living." The names Chestnut Flats, Cosby, Eagle Creek, and Cataloochee all became synonymous with moonshining and all the negative connotations that popular stereotypes promoted. Kephart wrote about accompanying federal revenue agents on a raid across the mountains into Tennessee and the reputation of the Sugarlands: "Sugarlands, a country of ill fame, hidden deep in remote gorges, difficult to access, tenanted by a sparse population who preferred to be a law unto themselves. For many a year it had been known as Blockader's Glory, which is the same as saying Moonshiner's Paradise, and we all believed it to be fitly named." Kephart did note the irony of North Carolinians—who had plenty of stills on their own side of the state line—disparaging the moonshiners of Tennessee when he concluded his statement with the words: "Thus doth sinless North Carolina look down upon sinful Tennessee."

Of course all stereotypes have some basis in fact and while the popular images of moonshiners exaggerated and often dehumanized mountain residents, the Great Smoky Mountains of the late 19th and early 20th centuries were awash in illegal corn liquor. Given the lack of records kept by people involved in illegal activity, it is hard to know the extent of the moonshine business in the region at this time or gauge its economic impact on the lives of Smokies residents. From available enforcement records and anecdotal evidence it appears that for a majority of residents—particularly in the more isolated sections of the region— participation in some aspect of moonshine production, transportation, distribution, or sale was as common an experience as plowing behind a mule.

During the challenging economic times of the late 1890s and early 1900s blockading did not make many Smokies residents rich, but it often provided an economic hedge and helped farmers stay at least marginally viable. The supplemental income illegal liquor provided helped pay taxes and allowed the purchase of at least some of the newly available consumer goods that railroads brought to the region. There are always costs to engaging in illegal enterprises, but for many residents of the Smokies, it was honest work and the costs were worth the benefits. As Charles Thompson observed, "It was illegal money—that much is true—but it was money made from sweat. That sweat money made liquor bosses rich, but it also bought and preserved small farms, keeping people out of mills and mines and on their own land for a generation or two longer, leaving people some independence to determine their own direction and to change their families' futures ultimately."

CHAPTER 4

PROHIBITION AND OTHER INCENTIVES

While local and statewide prohibition caused a boom in the production of blockade whiskey in the Smokies, it was small in comparison to the explosive growth and total transformation of the business that came when the 18th Amendment became the law of the land in 1919. New production methods and technologies allowed many blockaders to put the 40- to 50-gallon copper pot still in the barn next to the spinning wheel they no longer used and start making whiskey in huge stills capable of producing 500 or more gallons at a run. What had once been a craft, now became an industrial process. A pronounced division of labor came into being that tied together families, communities, towns, and whole counties and included, and implicated, women, children, young men, middle-aged men, the elderly, poor farmers, ambitious rural entrepreneurs, ruthless liquor kingpins, local store owners, and even bankers. Whereas in the early years of the 20th century Smokies moonshiners had developed markets in the small county-seat towns and milltowns and even in growing regional centers such as Asheville and Knoxville, in the 1920s and '30s illegal liquor flowed out of the Smokies to cities across the nation. What had generally been transported in horse-drawn wagons now sped out of the Smokies on myriad new county and state roads and highways in high-powered automobiles or in trucks under loads of farm produce. Some blockaders even employed airplanes to get their product to distant markets.

After the advent of national prohibition, a gallon of liquor that had recently yielded seventy-five cents to a dollar in profit could bring three to six dollars. Even small producers could net a thousand dollars or more for a few weeks' work. In addition, moonshine from the Smokies, made famous by the local color writers and more recent works like Kephart's *Our Southern Highlanders,* had *catchet* and was even more marketable across the country than run-of-the-mill bathtub gin. In the face of on-going poverty and worsening economic conditions for Smokies residents as the Great Depression hit, the money proved irresistible. As a Cherokee County, North Carolina moonshiner noted, "Everybody was needy; half of them didn't have shoes. I finally got to where I just didn't care. Young and stout and couldn't get jobs . . . . And I started making liquor. I had to have some money."

Skyrocketing demand helped create revolutionary changes in moonshine making in the Smokies, including the first major modification in the recipe for liquor since the blockaders' ancestors arrived in America and began distilling corn. Moonshiners discovered that by using refined sugar in their mash, and just a little corn meal, they could shorten the time period of fermentation by three-fourths and dramatically increase the volume that an individual blockader could produce. According to local legend, a moonshiner in Greene County, Tennessee first started to produce what became known as "sugar liquor" at his Paint Creek still in 1913. While it is hard to verify this story, by the time national prohibition hit and demand and prices skyrocketed, huge stacks of refined sugar began appearing in country stores throughout the region and demand for corn by distillers dropped off considerably. As Joseph Dabney observed, "For only $5 worth of sugar—100 pounds worth—the moonshiner could turn out ten gallons of high proof 'shine, selling for $20 to $40 a gallon."

Moonshiners in the Smokies further boosted their profits by modifying the traditional recipe further. Some added blocks of baker's yeast to the mash to speed the process of fermentation even more. In order to stretch a run further, many blockaders began cutting the proof of their whiskey. To mask this, they added adulterants such as glycerin— known as "beading oil"—that would make the product bead like high

A small still like this could easily be concealed in the fastness of the mountain wilderness. Some stills were even buried underground or hung in trees. Of course fire was a requirement for distilling, so smoke was often the clue that betrayed their locations.

proof whiskey. Others stooped to even lower depths by adding lye or even buckeyes to give their liquor an artificial bead. Some producers dumped in pepper, ginger, or tobacco to give their liquor some "sting" and the taste of high proof.

In addition to modifications in the basic recipe, the technology of stills also changed dramatically with the increased demand. While small-time moonshiners continued to produce much of the liquor in the region in 40-to 50-gallon copper stills, more and more big operators employed highly efficient and much larger plants. Some Smokies producers adopted the steamer still, a type developed and most commonly used in and around Wilkes County, North Carolina and often referred to as a "Wilkes-type" still. Steamer stills greatly shortened the time needed for distillation by adding a steam plant, generally made by welding together two sealed, steel 55-gallon oil drums. The lower drum served as a fire chamber, while the upper drum was filled with water. A pipe with a release valve connected the upper drum to the still and instead of building a fire under the still, the blockaders ran hot steam from the steam plant through the mash quickly distilling it. An added attraction for the steamer still was that, unlike traditional pot stills with the heat source under the still pot, the mash never scorched or stuck to the bottom. As North Georgia moonshiner Hubert Howell told Joseph Dabney, "It's the best they are. Steamer still whiskey is never burned. Ain't got no burnt taste." The fact that the heat source was not under the still also allowed Smokies distillers to use cheaper materials for their still pots, even wooden barrels, instead of copper. A big disadvantage to this type of still was that they rarely had pressure gauges or pressure release valves and steam boilers under high pressure could explode. This added new dangers to the business.

Most commonly in the Smokies however, the big moonshiners used huge pot stills of up to 1,000 gallons capacity. With these extra-large stills, blockaders were able to ferment their mash in the still pot itself, eliminating the need for mash barrels or boxes, decreasing the labor involved, and greatly speeding the process. This type of still became common in Cocke County and was traditionally made of copper. In the 1950s, when the price of copper rose dramatically and law enforcement got busy "cutting down" a significant number of stills, the local moonshiners began making them out of galvanized steel. With their huge size and shiny appearance, these stills became commonly known as the "Cosby Silver Cloud."

Other innovations during the Prohibition period further speeded the process, made it cheaper, helped producers keep up with their competitors, and increased profit margins. Moonshiners added heater boxes where they ran the alcohol vapor through a barrel containing cold mash before running it into the condenser, thus heating up the mash before it went into the still. They also employed mechanical pumps to move the mash from fermenter boxes to heater boxes and then into the still. Some Smokies moonshiners replaced copper condensers or worms with car or truck radiators because of their cheapness and increasing availability. Indeed, making moonshine, even in the remote hollows of the Smokies, quickly became more mechanized and shaped by modern industrial processes and technology rather than traditional knowledge.

This industrialized process also demanded more labor and cost-effective fuels. The plentiful hardwoods in the region still provided most of the fuel for small, seasonal blockaders, but many high-volume producers used coke, a fuel commonly used in steel production made by processing coal into a hotter-burning, relatively smokeless product. Piles of coke for sale began appearing regularly outside country stores throughout the region. Other moonshiners preferred some form of natural gas, another fuel that produced little smoke and whose temperature was easier to control.

The marketing and distribution of the millions of gallons of moonshine produced in the Smokies during the 1920s and '30s also changed with the national demand produced by Prohibition. In the early 20th century, illegal distillers traditionally sold their liquor locally, with some going to growing regional centers. But after 1920, Smokies moonshine found its way into cities across the country, particularly in the Northeast and Upper Midwest. The rise of the "Good Roads" movement in the 1920s and the resultant construction of state and federally maintained highways interconnecting the nation facilitated more efficient and long distance distribution. Henry Ford's assembly line led to cheaper automobiles and trucks to haul liquor to market and the rise of criminal syndicates in the major markets streamlined distribution. Horace Kephart actually predicted these changes in distribution as Prohibition began in the early 1920s: "I used to think that good roads would help to check moonshining, by making it easier for mountain farmers to market their corn in bulk at a fair profit . . . . But I never dreamed in those days, that distilled corn juice would be retailing at ten to twenty dollars a gallon. As things are, our new highways will make the distant marketing of blockade liquor a veritable line of trade. 'Mountain dew' will be collected by fly-by-night cars and carried to a far extended market."

Smokies moonshine passed through many hands between the producers of blockade liquor in the Smokies and the drinkers in distant cities, and all took a cut of the profits. The sugar-liquor was generally shipped out in five-gallon glass jars called carboys or in steel cans. Once the product got to bootleggers in the cities for distribution, it was "parted out" in smaller containers, passed on to several other distributors, and finally made it to the consumer. Consumers generally bought the product by the shot in urban speakeasies or homes in poor areas known as "shot houses" where moonshine sold by the shot for as little as ten cents.

While some moonshiners claimed their sugar liquor made in a 500-gallon still was as good as the traditional, double-distilled, all-corn product made in a 40-50-gallon copper-pot still, the vast separation between production and consumption led many Smokies moonshiners to worry little about the taste of their product or the side-effects of adding adulterants or condensing the product through a car radiator. Residents of the Smokies referred to the resulting product of distilled sugar, various adulterants, and even lead acetate leached into the alcohol from car radiators, as "pop skull," "bust head," "bumblings," or "jakeleg," referring to the headaches, fuzziness, and tremors that often accompanied the consumption of the product. In some African-American neighborhoods—where a considerable amount of sugar liquor was sold—the product was known as "splo," evidently short for "explosive," and sold for as little as fifteen cents per half-pint.

Not all Smokies moonshiners—or even most—adulterated their liquor, but practically all primarily distilled sugar and the product was inferior. For the blockaders themselves, in the words of Roy Brown of Cosby, "It was selling whiskey, and it was unfit to drink." As the authors of the *Foxfire* books observed, "It apparently is not that difficult to get away with making bad whiskey, because most of it is sold through bootleggers who themselves don't know where it came from. In addition, much of it is shipped to poorer districts of some of the bigger cities, and the people who buy it there have no means of finding out who

61

made it. Thus the operator of the still is reasonably safe, rarely having to pay for his sloppiness." As Charles Thompson noted, "Prohibition was not making the liquor business go away, it was just making it bad." After a visit to Cocke County in 1940, journalist Ernie Pyle observed the changes that had occurred in the illegal liquor business due to Prohibition: "The famous old mountain corn whiskey, which many a connoisseur still says is better than your bonded stuff, had almost gone out of existence. It took too long to make, and there was no market for such a high-class product."

While enforcement of the law on the federal level remained in the hands of the Department of Treasury, the government created a new agency—the Bureau of Prohibition—to attempt to keep the country dry. The agency got off to a slow start and always played catch-up as production of moonshine exploded in the Smokies. Many of the agents of the old Alcohol Tax Unit moved into the Bureau of Prohibition and the normal rules of the game between moonshiners and federal agents generally prevailed. As J. Carroll Cate, chief enforcement agent for the Bureau of Prohibition in Cocke County recalled, "You wouldn't want to meet finer people. They were honest and honorable. Just poor people. I've turned many a widow loose and never made a report. I did it because if I had, her children would have had no food." Many of the individuals who Cate sent to prison came by his office to visit after they had "built their time" in the federal penitentiary at Chillicothe, Ohio. Cate even lent them money to get started again—hopefully not back in the blockade business.

Apparently, the affection and respect was mutual. Ernie Pyle recounted in a nationally syndicated column after riding through Cocke County for a day with Cate: "You'd think a man who had put a lot of people behind bars wouldn't be coming back to his old haunts without a little shaking of knees, but I rode all day with Cate, and his visit was like a homecoming." Cate and Pyle visited the home of a woman who had been known in the area as "Queen of the Moonshiners." The woman insisted on having them stay for dinner and went out and killed a chicken. Pyle heard the woman tell Cate, "Everybody always liked you up here. You played square with us." The key to good relations according to Cate, "was to tell the truth when the case came to court. If, just to get a conviction, you testified to something the men knew was a lie, then your name was mud."

While making and selling liquor was also illegal by state law in North Carolina and Tennessee, local officials made only occasional busts—often near election time to cater to the town folks—but generally turned a blind eye to the business. Justice of the Peace Jim Hannah in Cataloochee "never considered it [folks in the community making moonshine] any of his part." Robert Woody of the same area recalled that locally, "officers of the law did not make themselves a nuisance." Mark Hannah recounted a scene he witnessed in Cosby in 1929 of a group of men loading cases of blockade liquor into a car "just as fast as they could . . . right in the middle of the road." Sitting on the bank overlooking the scene sat the high sheriff "with a badge on." When Hannah asked the men about this curious scene they responded that, "they made him drunk first thing so they could load." In addition, "The deputy sheriff was sittin' up on the bank drunker'n any of 'em." Local law enforcement who did try to enforce prohibition laws drew resentment and less cooperation from moonshiners than federal agents did. In the words of Doyle Webb, folks felt like the Prohibition Bureau agent was "simply doing a job he was paid to do," while local sheriff's deputies had lots of other duties and "were unfairly harassing the moonshiners."

With the higher profits and higher stakes that came with Prohibition era moonshining, however, blockade-related violence did escalate in the Smokies. Kephart noted the changed scene when he wrote a revised version of *Our Southern Highlanders* in 1922: "The greater the reward in sight, the greater risks will be run for it. The blockaders are getting ugly. Arrests have rapidly increased since prohibition, and so have mortal combats between officers and outlaws. Spies are everywhere and a hated gendarmerie patrols the country. The war between enforcement agents and blockaders is more widespread and deadly than ever before in our history. We who live in the mountains are fairly within gun-crack of it."

Violence within the community increased as well, particularly revenge shootings and killings of real, or perceived, informants. Quill Rose's nephew and namesake, Aquilla Eagleton "Eagle" Rose, was shot in the back of the head with a shotgun by men in Graham County, North Carolina who believed—erroneously—that he had informed on them. The murderers hid Eagle's body in Yellow Creek and it was not found for forty days. Authorities never tried or convicted anyone for the crime.

The organization of the blockade liquor business also extended to informal—and even formal—warning systems. In addition to the traditional methods of warning moonshiners by firing gunshots or sounding hunting horns, some folks took to the telephones or, in some extreme cases, set off dynamite. Ernie Pyle recounted the common use of dynamite in the Cosby section of Cocke County in his syndicated "Rambling Reporter" column in October, 1940: "One man lies along the one road that leads into the moonshining hills. When a car goes past, he jerks out his dynamite, throws it into the road, and off she goes. You can hear the boom for miles around. Much farther than you could hear a gunshot. And a minute or two after the first explosion, dynamite blasts start going off in the timbered hills one after another, until the air is so full of noise you can't talk. This is the signal that carries to the farthest ridge of the highest mountain, and it means, 'Look out! The revenooers are coming.'" The warning allowed smaller producers to take apart their stills and hide the parts separately and larger producers to do their best to disguise their operations often hidden in some outbuilding on a farm. At the least, the warnings gave the blockaders time to get away from the still before agents arrived. They may have had their still destroyed, but they avoided arrest and stayed free to start up another still in a new location.

At the top of the ladder in the blockader ranks in the Smokies were a group of "kingpins" who controlled a considerable portion of the trade and profited the most. Higher profits also led to greater organization of the business in many communities. While most blockade liquor was still made by small producers alongside other family members, they more often sold their product to some large operators who hired others to transport the product to market. These kingpins were the ones most likely to have big distilling plants of their own as well and they hired both skilled, older distillers to run the operations and young men—preferably ones without a criminal record so they would receive less time in the penitentiary if arrested—to do the heavy lifting and take the biggest risks such as transporting liquor to market. Some of the individuals who made the most money in the business were those who provided finance capital, invested their profits in legitimate businesses, and never went near a still.

Given its favorable location in close proximity to a large market and a culture that had long prized whiskey making, the Cosby section produced an inordinate number of such "kingpins" and a huge amount of liquor at the height of Prohibition. Some observers asserted that transporters hauled one thousand gallons over winding mountain roads to Asheville on any given night. Much more went to Knoxville or up to Lexington, Louisville, or Cincinnati. The trade was so large that Pyle, and many other observers, called Cosby the "moonshine capital of America."

The two best known of Cosby's liquor barons were Dick Denton and Ike Costner, although Robert Gunter was known as a "big man" in the business as well. As Denton's son, Hooper recalled, "My father was what I like to think of as the 'king' of the whiskey business." Denton had an outgoing personality, had a "good relationship" with a number of local Prohibition—and later Alcohol Tax Unit—agents, and was a major player in local and statewide Democratic Party politics. Denton's "good relationship" with federal agents did not keep him out of prison, however. Indeed, the price of being a "kingpin" in his case was to spend numerous terms in the penitentiary. Denton "built time" in federal penitentiaries in Atlanta, Chillicothe, Ohio, and Pennsylvania, as well as Tennessee's Brushy Mountain State Prison.

While there were definite benefits to being a big man in the liquor business in the Smokies, the costs of the elder Denton's decision to become a liquor kingpin had its effects on his family as well. Dick, Jr. recalled one incident where three armed men came to his house posing as federal agents. When the family allowed them in, the men pulled their guns, made them lie on the floor, and ransacked the house. This was not an unusual occurrence as people knew—because of federal banking laws that required banks to report large cash deposits—that blockading was a cash business and the kingpins had to keep a lot of it at hand making them attractive targets for thieves. Dick, Jr. well remembered the impact of such occurrences and the fear and uncertainty that came with being the son of a blockader: "It wasn't unusual, often, for me to be awakened during the night with someone wanting to purchase whiskey, or for that matter, awakened by an Alcohol Tax Unit man with a search warrant wanting to go through our house. It was a frightening experience, sometimes anyway. I don't know how many times I was frightened for my life."

Perhaps the most famous of the Cosby moonshiners was Ike Costner. As a young man, Costner left Cocke County and went to work in a cotton mill. When he heard stories of his friends making $3,000 a month in the blockade liquor business, he came home, learned how to make it, and soon became a top producer. He discovered, however, that his talents lay in organizing the business and increasingly bought his moonshine from small producers and shipped it out of the county. Costner and his associates drove around the county picking up sacks of jars filled with moonshine left by farmers at the edge of their fields and leaving the cash to pay for it behind. Like many in the business, by the 1920s Costner learned to love fast cars, always had "seven or eight in his yard," and even kept a skilled mechanic on retainer to keep them in "top condition and ready to roll." He often sent cars out loaded with 180 gallons of whiskey—which would net $500 at an urban market—accompanied by an empty car. The job of the empty car was to attract the attention of any law enforcement watching the roads, then speed off

Left: Ike Costner's U.S. Navy photo. Below: Ike was super-imposed in this family portrait because he was in jail. From left to right, Isaac Alan Jr. (Al), Beulah Hurst, and daughters Jean and Dorothy.

67

leading the officers on a chase in an opposite direction and allowing the loaded car to proceed on to market unmolested. Costner's business got so big that he and his men hauled liquor not only in fast cars, but in tractor trailer loads, and even in an airplane that took off and landed at a small Cosby airstrip (piloted by Clerc Baxter) to deliver Cosby moonshine as far away as Chicago.

Costner, like Denton, had powerful friends, but he also paid a high price for his activities. He once told an interviewer that Cocke County Sheriff Mack Harper did not go after him "because the District Attorney and the Judge was my friends. I had the county sewed up." Despite these connections, he spent a significant portion of his life in prison, served ten years in the Atlanta penitentiary for robbing a mail truck on its way to the Federal Reserve Bank at Charlotte, North Carolina of $100,000, spent six years in Alcatraz, nine years at Leavenworth Prison in Kansas, and several shorter stints at various state and federal prisons. While in prison, Costner did use his time well taking correspondence courses in business management, business administration, and flora culture and became an accomplished "jailhouse lawyer." Despite these long periods of incarceration, however, he remained an unrepentant moonshiner until his death well into his eighties. He attributed his long life to the fact that, unlike many blockaders, he imbibed in moonshine only occasionally, and never to excess.

As in Denton's case, Costner's chosen profession took a toll on his family. His daughter Jean Costner Schilling recalled: "We never knew when trouble would come. Suddenly there would be gunfire and bullets breaking the windows. Mom would yell, 'protect yourselves,' and we'd get under the bed or barricade ourselves some way. Or, we'd come home from church to find that the house had been broken into, with our furniture and clothing ripped and torn up. Enemies of my father thought he had tons of cash stashed away. But all we had was the house he had provided, before he was taken away." Costner's wife finally had enough, divorced him, and later married his mechanic.

In places like Cosby and Cocke County, such widespread and

large-scale operations had a major impact on the entire economy. Small farmers made needed cash by firing up their stills in the off-season and making a few runs of liquor to sell to the likes of Ike Costner. Young men made more money than they ever could on the farm hauling sacks of sugar into still sites, carrying the finished product out and then driving it to market, and found excitement in a testosterone-filled world of high-speed car chases, firearms, and dynamite. Those with metal-working skills particularly profited from the increased business that Prohibition brought. Still maker Thee King in North Georgia estimated he made over 800 stills, ranging in size from 25 to 135 gallons, between 1928 and 1940. He charged a dollar a gallon with the moonshiner providing all the copper sheeting and rivets. In Cataloochee, Raymond Caldwell recalled that "Major" Woody developed quite a reputation in the community for his metal work "because he had experience from puttin' the moonshine stills together." Store owners made significant profits selling 100-lb. sacks of sugar, yeast, cans, canning jars, and coke. Gay Webb, a storeowner in Cosby, asserted, "Back in the day, you were either a moonshiner, you supplied a moonshiner, or you were a preacher." Of course odds were that at least a part of the tithes and offerings that paid the preacher came from the proceeds of the blockade liquor business.

Cash made from illegal enterprises also flowed into other areas of the economy purchasing everything from crackers to cars. One matter that is hard to quantify is the amount of illegal money used as investment capital in purchasing farms and real estate or investing in legitimate businesses. It seems likely that given the amount of liquor produced and sold in the Smokies during Prohibition, a good deal of cash went to subsidize and create all kinds of business enterprise.

Children even benefitted from doing business with the moonshiners. Clyde Bell remembered growing up in Cosby picking blackberries and blueberries to sell to local blockaders. "They was always a market for something that you could make liquor from and brandy was more expensive than white lightning moonshine . . . . Over the summer we picked hundreds of gallons and we were paid 10 cents a gallon bucket. That's the way we got our shoes for the new school year." Vole Mathes started working at eight or nine when he "got old enough to be of use to the moonshiners." Having learned the trade he started making it himself when he "was strong enough to carry two sacks of sugar, one on each shoulder."

While blockading during Prohibition did have a salutary effect on many small farmers, and made a small minority wealthy, such widespread illegal activity took its toll on Smokies communities. Taking the step into one illegal business, in some cases, led those involved in illegal liquor into other illegal behavior. Rural speakeasies often became havens for prostitution, gambling, cockfighting, gunplay, and knifings. In addition, the high profits of the Prohibition era fueled a culture of political corruption in several Smokies counties that negatively affected them for generations. These counties' tax bases also suffered as so much productive capacity was untaxed and schools and infrastructure suffered.

Moonshining in the Smokies during the years of national Prohibition from 1919 to the repeal of the 18th amendment in 1933 had its costs and its benefits. The small farmer who occasionally made a run of corn liquor in his 40-to 50-gallon still did not get rich in the business

A moonshiner at work in the Cosby area.

and probably only realized a dollar or two profit per gallon. In addition, as Charles Thompson observed, "They took the risk, putting their land and life on the line every day, but didn't share the profits fairly. In the cities, liquor sold for up to ten or even twenty dollars a gallon. But there were middlemen, price gougers, big shots, and profiteers between mountain stills and city consumers." At the same time, it is hard to know how many men—and women—were able to pay their taxes, mortgages, store bills, even contribute a little to their church, and hold onto their land and their pride by "makin' a little likker."

The benefits for the kingpins—at least the ones whose stories have been recorded—were much more temporary. In the short term, they had lots of cash, fast cars, lived "high on the hog" and even possessed considerable political influence. They also, at least temporarily, injected lots of cash and employment into communities suffering from the severe economic downturn that affected the rural communities that predominated in the Smokies in the 1920s and '30s. In the long term, they spent their lives looking over their shoulder with the ever present danger of being arrested or killed in a shoot-out with law enforcement or some rival trying to take their business or their cash. They all experienced long periods away from family, friends, and community "building time" in the penitentiary. While Ike Costner did live a long life, his activities cost him his wife and limited his contact with his children. Dick Denton did not fare as well. He was shot in the back by another moonshiner in 1962, leaving him an invalid until he died two years later.

Whatever its costs and benefits, the moonshine business changed dramatically during the years of national Prohibition. The craft of distilling corn in a small copper pot still was pretty much dead except for a few folks who continued to make liquor the old way for their own consumption and for friends and neighbors. Almost all the liquor in the Smokies by the late 1920s was mostly distilled sugar with very little, if any, corn in the mix and likely as not made in a huge still fueled by coke or gas. Instead of hauling it to relatively local markets in horse-drawn wagons, the shine came out of the Great Smoky Mountains in souped-up cars, farm trucks, airplanes, and late in the period, tractor-trailers. While outsiders characterized moonshine making as a holdover from a more primitive, pioneer existence, in reality almost overnight it had become a modern, integrated, industrial process. And in most of the counties of the Smokies, it probably employed more people and made more profit than any other business in the region.

CHAPTER 5

MOONSHINER VS. REVENUER:
HIGH STAKES CAT-AND-MOUSE

The 1933 ratification of the 21st amendment to the U.S. Constitution repealing Prohibition brought some changes to the blockade liquor business in the Smokies, but it did not dislodge the moonshine business from its important economic and social niche. Demand for the product would never be as high again as the national market disappeared and prices immediately dropped from as high as $20 to as low as $2 per gallon. However, local demand for illegal liquor remained high due to the persistence of local option laws that kept much of the region legally "dry," in most cases into the '60s. In addition, the Great Depression continued to cause economic hardship on the farm, prompted folks who had moved away and lost their jobs in industry to move back in with family, and created the type of economic desperation that led normally law-abiding folks into illegal enterprises. While the moonshine business was smaller than in the Prohibition era, and the processes of production and distribution remained relatively the same, it continued for many years to supplement the income of some folks in the region and fuel some sizeable operations for years to come.

One major change that had an impact on illegal liquor production in the region was the establishment of Great Smoky Mountains National Park and—at least technically—the removal of hundreds of thousands of acres of land that once harbored many a moonshine still. While the park was not established officially until 1933, the National Park Service appointed Ross Eakin as superintendent in 1931. Eakin hired four rangers to attempt to patrol the huge, and growing, area, to protect the

The national park's first superintendent, Ross Eakin, encouraged his rangers to use sensitivity when enforcing laws against moonshiners.

flora and fauna, put out forest fires, and prevent illegal behavior on the land, including the production of blockade liquor. In the early years, this process was further complicated by the fact that hundreds of families remained on park land on leases and continued to farm, although with strict limitations on their use of the land. Of course, some of these farmers supplemented their income by making a little moonshine.

Eakin and his rangers had a delicate situation on their hands, as the removal of families from the Smokies to make way for the park had angered many individuals in the region and become a political hot potato. Eakin encouraged his rangers to handle confrontations over moonshining with diplomacy to avoid further angering the local communities. While park officials made it clear they would not tolerate moonshining in the park, the tendency was to warn folks to enable them to dismantle and remove a still before rangers destroyed it. Audley Whaley, warden in the eastern end of the park in the moonshine hotbeds of Cataloochee, Big Creek, and Cosby, asserted, "Most of the time if I found a still I'd leave a note on it and tell them to get it out by a certain date or we'd take care of it." Charles Dunn took a more aggressive stance in the Cades Cove area he patrolled and believed the Park Service needed to send a stronger message. In 1931, he encountered three men setting up a still in an abandoned cabin, ordered them out, and burned the cabin—still and all—to the ground. One thing Dunn, or any ranger for that matter, did not do was arrest any of the men. Indeed, while Eakin recorded the capture or destruction of hundreds of stills—as many as twenty a month—in his monthly Superintendent's Reports sent to National Park Service headquarters, the standard phrase "the owner of the still was not apprehended" almost always appeared afterward.

Leaseholders who persisted in making liquor on park property did suffer direct consequences from Park Service officials in being forced to give up their leases and move out of the park. In his May 1931, report Eakin wrote, "Some undesirable characters were notified to move from the park by November 1. Letters written to them stated if they or any of their families were in court [for moonshining] before that time they would be requested to move immediately." Eakin explained the November 1 deadline as allowing the miscreants enough time "to harvest their crops." While Eakin and his rangers did order people out, they most often took a less confrontational approach as they did with Les Williamson in 1932. Rangers

By the 1960s rangers were showing less sensitivity, especially towards large-scale moonshiners. Here rangers Whaley and Penny destroy two 500-gallon moonshine stills beside Roostertown Branch near Cosby.

confiscated "a crude affair constructed of a 50-gallon oil drum . . . capable of turning out high powered liquor" that Williamson and his sons operated in the Smokemont area. Rangers contacted him and encouraged him to "vacate his leasehold." If he did so "by the end of the month, no charges would be brought against him or his boys."

Although Alcohol Tax Unit agents had jurisdiction in the park, rangers made it clear to leaseholders, local residents, and to ATU agents themselves that the ranger's job was to enforce park rules and not to enforce federal revenue laws. When a local ATU agent asked Audley Whaley if he'd seen any "suspicious activity," Whaley replied, "I'll do my job without your help and you do yours without mine." The unofficial policy of the Park Service did get them in trouble on occasions with the ATU who did not appreciate their approach. In July 1932, ATU officials accused a Cosby area ranger of being "in sympathy with moonshiners." Superintendent Eakin tasked Assistant Chief Ranger Charles Dunn to conduct an investigation and he found the charges "groundless." Eakin later reported, "It is my opinion their charges were the result of a grudge and when I refused to discharge our patrolman without an investigation, they were through."

While they were circumspect in how they did it, the Park Service did realize some material benefits from cracking down on moonshine activities in the park. Eakin assigned the job of collecting artifacts reflective of mountain culture for a future museum to rangers H. C. Wilburn and Charlie Grossman. The pair confiscated a number of intact stills they considered "good specimen[s] for museum purposes." In 1931, Smokies rangers presented a small still to Secretary of the Interior Ray Lyman Wilbur who took it back to Washington "as a souvenir of the Great Smokies." Rangers also confiscated vehicles used in moonshine operations in the park and repurposed them. Charlie Bell told an interviewer that the Park Service "captured" a 1933 Hudson Terraplane used to haul moonshine in the park. Rangers "painted it Park Service green, put Department of the Interior tags on it" and Bell and Charlie Grossman used it for a patrol car.

The Civilian Conservation Corps assigned thousands of young men to work in the Smokies, and once again the local market for moonshine boomed.

Despite the limiting factor that the coming of the national park had on whiskey production in the Smokies, it also had its benefits for local producers. With the removal of most of the population, there were plenty of places to hide a small, mobile distilling operation on the fringes of the park. Eakin often noted the commonality of this in his reports from the 1930s and early 1940s where rangers destroyed a large number of 40- to 50-gallon stills. Of course rangers did not get to most of the stills given that the park was so huge and the number of rangers so small. In a 1931 report Superintendent Eakin expressed his frustration with this situation in his monthly report: "It is physically impossible for 4 men to protect 300,000 acres, especially when it is considered that there is a dense population around the park and many people are residing in the park." While the numbers of rangers did increase through the 1930s, the size of the park did as well, reaching almost 500,000 acres by the end of the decade. The Depression years also provided a new local market for Smokies moonshiners within the park in the thousands of young men brought in from across the country to work in the Civilian Conservation Corps camps. While liquor was banned in the camps, both the blockaders and the CCC boys found ways to sell and buy moonshine and Park Service reports contain accounts of enrollees being charged with both possession and "transporting untaxed liquor."

Smokies blockaders also still had plenty of market demand for their product in the growing cities in the Southeast, especially when World War II sparked unprecedented economic growth due to the millions of dollars spent on defense industries and the location of military bases in the region. War did create some problems for liquor producers in the region because the draft took many of the young men—who did the heavy lifting and risky hauling—off to the armed forces and led to rationing of sugar, gasoline, tires, and copper.

The skyrocketing demand for cheap—or any for that matter—liquor on military bases and in the cities and the decreasing priority of local liquor law or federal liquor tax enforcement more than made up for the difficulties producers faced. Because many blockaders had extensive criminal records, draft boards declared them "4-F" and "not acceptable for military service." Meanwhile their counterparts in law enforcement were prime candidates for the draft. The Army, at the insistence of General George C. Marshall, later in the war changed the Selective Service rules to allow men to serve who had only one "liquor-related offense" and who were no longer on probation. However, in the mountains, blockaders far outnumbered enforcement officials. Besides, with a world at war, enforcing liquor laws was nowhere near the top of the list for local or federal officials. North Georgia moonshiner John Henry Chumley commented on the lack of law enforcement and the benefits to blockaders: "There was lots of likker making then and the law didn't fool with it. They didn't fool with nobody. Didn't hardly ever hear of a still getting' cut nowheres."

Entrepreneurial moonshine makers found creative ways to deal with supply and distribution challenges. In fact, with their experience in the illegal liquor business, moonshine producers in the Smokies found it relatively easy to operate black market smuggling operations to get the supplies they needed. They also found ways to "make do" especially in dealing with the sugar shortage. Smokies blockaders created a regular pipeline from Georgia to haul syrup made from sorghum as a substitute for sugar. When they could not even get syrup, they reverted to the old ways of using corn malt and more corn in the mash. As Hamper McBee, who made liquor during the period on the Cumberland Plateau of Tennessee recalled, "Back during World War II, when there was a shortage of sugar, lots of straight pure corn was made." While the traditional recipe required much more time, wartime profits made it worthwhile. Indeed, while few Smokies moonshiners have talked about their experience during the war, in more candid moments they have admitted that they made more money during the early 1940s than even the heyday of Prohibition.

After the war, demand for mountain moonshine remained high as most counties and municipalities in the region maintained their dry status—often with the aid of the votes of moonshiners. Industry and urban areas grew and the economy boomed. The federal liquor tax skyrocketed, making the illegal product much cheaper even when folks could purchase the legal product. At this time, the illegal liquor business entered what might be termed its *Thunder Road* era, with the preferred method of delivering moonshine in the region becoming the jacked-up, high-powered automobile. Because it took Detroit a while to resume a high level of production while they re-tooled from making tanks and jeeps to making passenger cars, the liquor runners often relied on pre-war makes. Most popular was Henry Ford's last great invention; the flat-head, V-8 Ford. Haulers especially liked the 1939-40 era coupes. When the seats and trunk wall were taken out they could hold up to twenty-two six-gallon cases of liquor.

During this time period, skilled automobile mechanics became as prized in the Smokies as accomplished metal workers. As long as they could keep their mouth shut and did not ask a lot of nosy questions, mechanics could make a very good living boring out the engines of cars, adding additional carburetors or even superchargers, or installing heavy truck springs and shocks to make a fully loaded liquor hauler remain stable on curvy mountain roads. As ATU agent Bill Griffin, who covered Cocke County, recalled, "the moonshiners built some good, high performance cars . . . . What they had was far superior to what we had." Griffin recalled that the moonshiners' unmuffled cars, "Made a helluva noise. You could hear those things for miles on a clear night." As legendary Atlanta mechanic Red Vogt—who worked on cars for both law enforcement and the bootleggers—asserted, the reason the blockaders got the best cars was "because they paid cash."

To evade law enforcement the young liquor haulers needed more than a high-powered V-8 Ford; they needed the nerve and skill to push that car to its very limits. Before getting behind the wheel of a fully-loaded car headed for market, they learned how to powerslide through the turns on dirt roads and how to execute the 180 degree "bootleg turn" without ending up on their roof. On occasions, Griffin would hide out and watch Cocke County liquor drivers practice: "Those kids practiced like mad. I've laid up there many a night on the side of the mountains watchin' 'em practice spin-outs and turns . . . evasive maneuvers and escape maneuvers."

Drivers also equipped their cars with special features that further helped them evade capture. Some traveled with boxes of tacks to strew on the road behind them if law enforcement pursued. Some fashioned devices to drop oil on the hot engine to produce a smoke screen while others had tanks that sprayed oil on the road to make their pursuers lose traction or wreck altogether. When federal agents devised a special device to the front of their cars to clamp down and hold the back bumper of a fleeing bootlegger car, the blockaders attached their rear bumpers with flimsy coat-hanger wire so law enforcement would end up only holding a bumper. By the 1950s, Smokies liquor runners also became pioneers in using scanners to monitor law enforcement and two-way radios to communicate with their partners in crime. Ray Brown of Cocke County attached a couple of railroad ties to the front of his 1940 Ford "for ramming through blockades" set up by enforcement officials.

While not as wild and woolly as depicted in movies like Robert Mitchum's *Thunder Road*, it was still an exciting scene for both the young

Hollywood fell in love with the drama between moonshiners and the law. Top: Actor and producer Robert Mitchum on the set of the movie Thunder Road *near Asheville, NC. Middle: Steamer-type still on the set of* Thunder Road. *Bottom: Silver cloud still tended by actor Trevor Bardette (Vernon Doolin) also from* Thunder Road. *Next page: An impressive display of stills confiscated by rangers and other law enforcement officers in the early years of the existence of Great Smoky Mountains National Park.*

81

Revenue officers and a still captured on Rich Mountain in 1931.

liquor runners and their pursuers. As federal revenue agent Bill Griffin recalled, "We were about as crazy as the damned moonshiners. A bunch of kids having a good time." Surprisingly, unlike the other three areas of the southern Appalachian region often referred to as "moonshine capitals"—Dawson County, Georgia, Franklin County, Virginia, and Wilkes County, North Carolina—the Smokies never produced any major NASCAR stars. In the 1950s and 1960s, the liquor-hauler ranks did, however, foster a fair share of local stars on the increasing number of dirt tracks that cropped up like mushrooms in a rainy season in Asheville, Maggie Valley, Newport, Bulls Gap, Maryville, and Knoxville.

On occasions, car chases got very serious, and even deadly, and neither side had a "good time." Some overzealous ATU agents began trying to shoot out the tires on the bootleggers' cars, but the practice was stopped after a few fatal accidents. As reporter Harold Julian observed, "Moonshining is illegal, but it's not a capital offense." Officials also used "stop strips" with nails sticking up out of a board laid across the road which could cause high speed liquor cars to crash violently, a tactic featured in *Thunder Road* and supposedly based on a true incident on Bearden Hill just to the west of Knoxville.

However, it was most often in everyone's best interests to keep the violence and mayhem to a minimum and make sure neither side wandered too far from the unwritten rules. When someone did stray over the line, the other side sent a strong message. According to Julian, a Cosby bootlegger once ran over a federal agent in making his escape. In retaliation, "Every available agent in the state swept into the area and began destroying stills." To stop this and restore some balance, area moonshiners "went into North Carolina, abducted the bootlegger who had fled, and brought him back, tied with ropes, to Cosby." Revenue agent Ray Cline recounted an occasion where a "bad egg" threatened to shoot any agent that tried to bust his still. Cline and others went to the man's house, called him out, and "talked to him long enough for neighbors to notice." The agents then proceeded to a neighbor's still they knew about and blew it up. In retaliation, people in the area quickly began informing the agents on the whereabouts of the "bad egg's" stills and he was soon arrested.

Most of the time the enforcement scene was mundane, boring, and far from exciting. Revenue agents spent a much greater amount of time in tromping through the woods trying to find stills than they did in high-speed car chases or shoot-outs. They talked to people in the community and tried to gain information. They laid in wait for hours on end and staked out still sites to catch people in the act, or sat on the side of a lonely country road waiting to see if some high-powered liquor car came. As Ray Cline recalled, "Agents were instructed to shoot only in self-defense or to protect someone else." Increasingly, they tried to catch moonshiners through more sophisticated means, most notably in tracking large sales of the sugar used to make the liquor. As Ernie Pyle observed, "The storekeepers were scared into making everybody who bought an excessive amount of sugar sign up for it, and the moonshiners wouldn't put their names down in that book where the revenuers would see it. So they couldn't get sugar. So they didn't make so much moonshine. See, it's simple. You don't even have to shoot anybody."

In actuality, it was not that "simple" for revenue agents as, in the eternal cat-and-mouse game played by revenue agents and moonshiners, the blockaders found ways around local suppliers. Big-time moonshiners often purchased whole tractor-trailer loads of sugar in Florida or Louisiana and hauled it back to the Smokies. According to sports reporter and biographer Tom Higgins, moonshiner and NASCAR legend Junior Johnson regularly split truckloads of sugar hauled from New Orleans with Cocke County blockaders.

Informers remained the best way for agents to find information, bust up stills, and arrest perpetrators. As Charles Riddle recalled, "Informers were very valuable. One good informer might be worth two or three agents. A new agent with new boots might walk six months and

Gun-weilding William 'Will Gull' Tipton and sidekick with a still they pre-sumably captured in the Cades Cove area.

not find a still." The incentive for most informers was often what got them into the moonshine business to begin with—the need for money. In the 1950s and '60s, agents paid up to $100 to informants, depending on the size of the still involved. On other occasions, agents offered arrested blockaders a deal in order to shorten their sentence. According to Riddle, "If you'll help us catch two or three others, we'll get your time cut." Agents also took advantage of family feuds, folks wanting revenge, or petty jealousy to gain information. Riddle reported that one moonshiner reported on a neighbor "because he admired the guy's wife. He thought he might make some time with her if the neighbor was in jail."

Concern that an angry neighbor might inform on them made folks in communities where moonshining was common anxious about maintaining good relations. As reporter Harold Julian observed, "Because of the fear one might squeal on the other, moonshining neighbors were extremely nice to each other . . . freely lending even still parts." Maintaining amicable relations also signaled to neighbors that you were not mad at them and therefore not a threat to inform. The problem of informants did keep Smokies communities on edge and, in many cases, on their best behavior. Their courtesy did not extend to unknown outsiders who were always treated with suspicion, at least until someone in the community could vouch that they were not with the government.

Moonshining remained a common feature of life until a number of factors helped change the economic incentives to make, sell, and transport illegal liquor in the Smokies. The coming of new industries—and expansion of existing ones—in the region in the 1950s and '60s created job opportunities that paid enough to make folks reconsider the hard work and stress that came with the blockade liquor business. As ATU agent Grant McGarity noted, "With more and more industries moving into the South, a lot of the old moonshiners simply found easier and better ways to make a living." With the increasing availability and relative cheapness of used automobiles, small farmers could now easily commute to places like the Stokely Brothers vegetable canning plant and Alcoa Aluminum in East Tennessee and Champion Fibre, Dayco Corporation, and Meade Paper in Western North Carolina. At the same time, with improvements in transportation and government stabilization of crop prices, small farmers could much more easily supplement their factory income by raising a little burley tobacco, cattle, or chickens. Such farmers in the Smokies had long used making moonshine to supplement their income and help pay their taxes. Now much of that supplemental income came from other, and much more legal, sources.

The increasing availability and relative cheapness of legal alcohol in the 1960s and '70s also took away a good deal of the moonshiner's market. In 1961, Knoxville voters ended local prohibition, closing the door—at least partially—on what Alex Gabbard called, "a vast market for moonshiners and bootleggers." By 1967, the city had 56 legal liquor stores. Other regional cities followed suit, although many of the rural counties of the Smokies remained at least partially dry for years, some up to the present day. Legal liquor also became increasingly cheap, because the federal excise tax did not increase between the mid 1950s and the mid 1980s.

At the same time, the costs of making liquor and the costs of being caught increased dramatically. As a former federal agent told Harold Julian, when the cost of sugar "skyrocketed" with institution of an embargo on Cuba and a high tariff on imported sugar in the 1960s, "That was the final blow. It put most of the rest of them out of business." Enforcement became tougher as well with agents using spotter planes and increased sentences from federal courts. The records of the Bureau of Alcohol Tobacco and Firearms—the former ATU, renamed in 1968—show the dramatic decline in the industry. In 1967, federal agents destroyed over 6,000 stills in the Southeast U.S., most of them in the southern Appalachian region. By 1977, the number had dropped to less than 500, and by 1997, only about 20 per year. By the mid 1970s the ATF had cut its enforcement staff from eight agents dedicated to Cocke Couty alone, to three agents stationed in Knoxville responsible for all of

The rising cost of sugar, the growing availability of inexpensive legal liquor, and improvements in law enforcement technologies inevitably made moonshiners a threatened species.

East Tennessee. While greatly diminished, moonshining persisted in the Smokies up to the present day. Some individuals continued making it, because that is what they knew and it was part of their family tradition. Homer Valentine of Cosby remained in what he called, "that fruit jar business" until his knees "got so bad I couldn't carry it." Even a few large-scale operations continued; for example, in 1975, officials busted an operation with a 15,277-gallon capacity still—the largest ever seized—in Jefferson County, Tennessee. Most of the remaining business is in small stills for very local markets, generally friends and neighbors. As one former federal agent noted in 1997, "You've got to feel around to find it anymore. I don't think you'll find too many people who'd sell it to you if they didn't know you. . . You just have to know where to look."

Even as moonshining began to die out, its mythological place in the Great Smoky Mountains remained, promoted by movies, television shows, and music that reinforced that myth. While the number of movies devoted to blockading never again matched the deluge of such films from the early years of the 20th century, moonshine generally appeared somewhere in films on the Smokies and the southern

Appalachian region. *Thunder Road*—written, produced, and starring Robert Mitchum in 1958—became the quintessential moonshiner film featuring a rural mountain culture steeped in illegal liquor, hopped-up cars, and high-speed chases on mountain roads. The film was largely filmed in Asheville, rural Buncombe County, Rutherford County, and Transylvania County, all in Western North Carolina. Mitchum even composed the theme song, "The Ballad of Thunder Road" which became a hit single.

The movie later became a cult classic, regularly screened at drive-in theaters around the Southeast into the 1970s and '80s, and still draws crowds to occasional screenings. *Thunder Road* prompted a number of imitators, particularly in the B-movie market that featured white lightning and fast cars including *White Lightning Road* and *Thunder in Carolina*. Although it featured a run of Coors Beer and not illegal liquor, the Burt Reynolds vehicle *Smoky and the Bandit* could be said to be the culmination of the genre.

Moonshining also became a staple in television shows that depicted the southern Appalachian region in the 1960s, '70s, and into the '80s. *The Andy Griffith Show* often featured stories of Andy and Barney tracking down mountain moonshiners like Rafe Hollister, Jubal Foster, or even respectable elderly women like Clarabelle and Jennifer Morrison. Moonshine themes also permeated

Even more so than Hollywood, folk singers and songwriters loved to celebrate the "romance" of the mountain moonshiner.

The Beverly Hillbillies, and formed the bedrock of the series plotline in
The Dukes of Hazzard.

No genre in popular culture was more saturated in white lightning
than country music. The earliest days of what was originally called
"Hillbilly Music" in the 1920s, featured stars such as Fiddlin' John
Carson, whose fictitious biography billed him as a North Georgia
moonshiner. His daughter Rosa Lee often accompanied him on guitar
and promoters gave her the stage name "Moonshine Kate." Gid Tanner
and the Skillet Lickers became stars as well, partly due to their image
as a bunch of fiddlin' and pickin' moonshiners as well as comedy skits
such as one entitled "A Corn Licker Still in Georgia." References to
moonshining also became staples in both songs and skits performed
in the popular new "barn dance" radio shows, most notably the Grand
Ole Opry. In 1959, the song "White Lightning"—written by J. P.
Richardson, a.k.a. the "Big Bopper"—became the first number one hit
recorded by George Jones and was later covered by country stars Waylon
Jennings, Johnny Paycheck, and Joe Diffie.

Bluegrass became the music genre that perhaps most celebrated
moonshine and moonshine culture. Bascom Lamar Lunsford of
Buncombe County, North Carolina wrote and recorded the classic tune
"Mountain Dew" in 1940. Bluegrass giants such as Mother Maybelle
Carter, Grandpa Jones, Doc Watson, and the Stanley Brothers, as well
as country star Willie Nelson, and even Johnny Cash in a duet with Bob
Dylan, later recorded it. The song, among other things, describes the
process of blind exchange, a method still commonly used to purchase
moonshine:

> There's a big hollow tree
> Down the road here from me
> Where you lay down a dollar or two.
> Then you go around the bend
> When you come back again
> There's a jugful of mountain dew.

91

The Andy Griffith Show brought the bluegrass group, "The Dillards" and their classic moonshining song "Dooley," to a national audience. The song describes Dooley as a loveable moonshiner just "tryin' to make a dollar." When Dooley dies "the men stood round and cried" at their loss and then "buried him on the mountain" where "they put a jug beside him, and a barrel for a stone."

Perhaps the most popular bluegrass song of all time ties the Smokies directly to the illegal liquor business. In 1967, Felice and Boudleaux Bryant—who lived in Gatlinburg at the time—wrote "Rocky Top," a song made popular by the Osborne Brothers and country star Lynn Anderson. In the early 1970s, the University of Tennessee's "Pride of the Southland" marching band started playing it at athletic events and the song has since become the official fight song for Volunteer athletics. Bluegrass audiences request the song so often that the Red Clay Ramblers composed a satirical favorite entitled, "Play 'Rocky Top' (or I'll Punch Your Lights Out)." Although ostensibly a tribute to country living, as opposed to the "cramped up city life," "Rocky Top" contains several references to moonshining including a verse on why folks on Rocky Top make liquor:

> Corn won't grow at all on Rocky Top
> Ground's too rocky by far
> That's why all the folks on Rocky Top
> Get their corn from a jar.

By the 1970s and '80s, however, moonshining was no longer the essential organ it had once been to the Smokies, but more like the human appendix, a holdover from a primordial past. Still the institution lived on with a few in the region who liked moonshine so much they had to keep making it, or who were so tied to their family's past activities, they did it to honor their ancestors. Very few made illegal liquor to support themselves.

CONCLUSION

MOONSHINE FOR THE MASSES

Ironically, a revival both in the fascination of the popular culture and in the actual production of corn liquor hit the Smokies beginning at the turn of the 21st century. People's interest in the subject was stimulated by a couple of unlikely characters who both reinforced and challenged the moonshiner stereotypes that developed over the years. In 2000, documentary filmmaker Kelly L. Riley released a short film entitled "Moonshine" featuring Graham County, North Carolina moonshiner Jim Tom Hedrick. Hedrick soon became an underground sensation and the film won numerous awards at film festivals around the country including the New England Film Video Festival and South X Southwest. Later, Jim Tom's fame increased as clips of the film became Youtube favorites. Hedrick first learned the trade from a group of older men in the 1960s who made moonshine inside Great Smoky Mountains National Park and kept at it over the years even though he "built some time" for his activities.

The film shows Jim Tom making liquor, drinking liquor, and talking and looking like someone you would expect to make illegal liquor—including having to blow into a breathalyzer so he can start his car. According to Jim Tom, he holds a North Carolina record with 21 DUIs and once hit a car head-on while driving a motorcycle at better than 100 m.p.h. He also sells model copper stills and even full-size forty-gallon stills, although of course he strongly cautions his buyers that these are not to be used for illegal purposes. In 2009, Riley made a sequel to his original film, also featuring Jim Tom, entitled "Still

Making Moonshine."

About the same time that Jim Tom became a sensation, an even more famous Smoky Mountains moonshiner, Marvin "Popcorn" Sutton, superseded him. Sutton split his time between Maggie Valley, North Carolina and Cocke County, Tennessee and was, at least, a third generation illegal liquor maker. In 1999, he self-published a book detailing his life as a moonshiner in the Great Smoky Mountains entitled *Me and My Likker*. He followed his book up with a decidedly amateur video with the same title instructing viewers on how to make moonshine, on the three varieties of moonshine—"fightin'," "lovin'," and "banjer pickin'"—, on how to judge the proof of liquor, and if they didn't already know, how to get drunk on it. All of this came with a banjo accompaniment provided by Sutton's buddy Leon Wells. Popcorn marketed his books and videos—and later souvenir t-shirts reading "Jesus turned the water into wine. I turned it into liquor. –Popcorn Sutton," at his Maggie Valley junk shop and in area restaurants, gas stations, and barber shops, but his fame was pretty local.

In 2008, Popcorn's notoriety went national. First, documentarian Neal Hutcherson released a film entitled *The Last One*, which followed Popcorn as he drove his Model-A Ford pick-up along dirt roads near Maggie Valley to locate the perfect still site, put together and build a furnace for a 40-gallon, copper-pot still, and (allegedly) make the "last damn run of likker" he'd "ever make." The film aired fairly widely, primarily on public television stations. Popcorn's popularity skyrocketed later in the year when the History Channel featured him in a documentary narrated by Billy Ray Cyrus entitled *Hillbilly: the Real Story*.

Popcorn gave his fans what they wanted: the quintessential, bearded, salty, overall and flannel-shirt wearing, "meddlin' guvmint"-hating, good-old-boy moonshiner topped off with a pork-pie hat with a raccoon's penis bone stuck through the crown. His *Me and My Likker*

Right: "Popcorn" Sutton went from a local character to a national celebrity in a very short time.

video had featured him making sugar liquor in a huge, 600-gallon, stainless steel, gas-fired, Cosby silver cloud still in some outbuilding on his farm. By the time *The Last One* and the History Channel came along, he had refined his image to depict himself as an old-time, copper-pot craftsman, making liquor the old-fashioned way up in a remote cove in the Smokies, the last of a dying breed. Like many other natives of the Great Smoky Mountains, Popcorn was very artful in figuring out what image of mountain people the world wanted and then happily selling it back to them.

Just as Popcorn reached the height of celebrity in the Smokies region, like many a tragic character, hubris brought it all crashing to an end. While tourists bought the occasional Popcorn t-shirt or clock, what everyone really wanted was genuine Popcorn-made moonshine. Sutton returned to cranking out the sugar liquor with a 1,000-gallon silver cloud still located on his Parrotsville, Tennessee farm and began to supply the demand. Of course, cultivating an image as an international media celebrity while trying to secretly run, market, and sell thousands of gallons of illegal liquor are incompatible goals. Sutton's friend Mark Ramsey warned him, "Old man, you can't be a movie star and make liquor too." Popcorn responded, "You can't sell it if no one knows you have it." However, federal authorities grew tired of Popcorn's open defiance of the law of the land and launched an undercover operation to catch him. In March 2008, they raided his Parrotsville property and agents discovered the 1,000-gallon capacity still and over 800 gallons of moonshine on hand. A subsequent raid of a storage unit in Maggie Valley netted agents another large still and a number of firearms, compounding the charges against him.

Sutton pleaded guilty to the charges and the judge sentenced him to 18 months in a federal penitentiary. At this point, Popcorn paid the ultimate penalty for his celebrity. He had sworn publicly that he would not go back to prison and—priding himself on being a man of his word—on March 16, 2009 committed suicide. He sent his wife Pam to the grocery store, ran a hose from the tailpipe into the backseat of his favorite car—a green 1960s Ford Fairlane that he had paid for with three gallons of moonshine—and cranked the car up. A public funeral held in October brought out a crowd of more than 350 people—including country music star Hank Williams, Jr.—, featured an antique hearse pulled by two black Percheron horses, a procession through Parrotsville, and private internment on the family property. His death was reported nationally and included an obituary in the *Wall Street Journal* and a later feature article in the *New York Times*. Popcorn's death has not taken his craggy visage out of the media spotlight as clips from *The Last One* are regularly included in the Discovery Channel reality show *Moonshiners* which follows the exploits of a couple of South Virginia blockaders and the law enforcement officials trying to track them down.

The moonshine business has also recently fed the tourism industry in the Smokies. In 2010, the Tennessee Department of Tourism Development created and began advertising a 200-mile auto tour that according to their website, follows "along the same route that rebel bootleggers used to transport their forbidden whiskey. Imagine the thrill of the bootleggers' chase, careening through the jagged mountains of the Upper Cumberland Region while outmaneuvering the long arm of the law."

This public fascination with moonshine and moonshiners in the Smokies inspired entrepreneurs to get in on the game and start producing "legal moonshine"—although technically if it's legal, it's not moonshine. Changes in laws in Tennessee and North Carolina in the 2000s, at least partially due to the wild success of micro beer breweries and wineries in the area, created a legal space for small whiskey distilleries. Ironically, the first person to step into that space in North Carolina with a corn liquor product was native New Yorker Joe Michalek who opened Piedmont Distillers in Madison (just north of Greensboro) in 2005 producing Catdaddy Carolina Moonshine. In 2007, Michalek partnered with NASCAR legend Junior Johnson to produce Junior Johnson's Midnight Moon. Since they started operations, Piedmont Distiller's moonshine business has taken off and their products are now

A recent change in state law allowed Sevier County, Tennessee locals Joe and Jessi Baker to parlay Joe's grandmother's family moonshine recipe into an immensely popular legal moonshine distillery.

available in forty-seven states.

When Tennessee liberalized its laws in 2009, Ole Smoky Distillery in downtown Gatlinburg was the first to begin making legal moonshine. Started by three native East Tennessee investors—two of them lawyers—who all claim a historic family connection to the illegal product, Ole Smoky not only produces un-aged corn whiskey, "moonshine cherries," apple pie moonshine, and a variety of seasonal flavors, but has also become one of the most popular tourist destinations on the Gatlinburg strip. They have since opened additional retail outlets and are building a second distillery two blocks from the original in downtown Gatlinburg. Ole Smoky's moonshine is currently distributed in thirty-seven states (including Hawaii) and is even available in selected Walmarts and Sam's Clubs.

Taking advantage of both the local foods movement and micro-brewery scene in Asheville, Troy & Sons Distillers became the first legal moonshine maker in the mountains of North Carolina in 2010. Using only open-pollinated, heirloom, Crooked Creek white corn, the husband and wife team of native Texans Charlie and Troy Ball produce what they like to call "keeper moonshine, the kind that never left the home place," that "any credible moonshiner would drink himself." In 2011, the Balls moved their operation from a barn on a local farm to the Highland Brewing Company facility in Asheville and started making their products in a 2,000-liter, Kothe still custom made in Germany. Unlike Piedmont and Ole Smoky, Troy & Sons' moonshine and its aged "Oak Reserve" corn whiskey are decidedly upscale products. In Charlie Ball's words, they consider it more of an "American grappa," and see their market as the trendy bars of South Beach or L.A., not the Gatlinburg tourists and NASCAR fans that Ole Smoky and Piedmont cater to. Feature stories on the distillery and its owners have appeared in *Garden & Gun* and *Southern Living* magazines and on MSNBC's "Morning Joe" and CBS's "This Morning."

Not surprisingly, in 2011, an enterprising Californian and former professional motorcyle racer named Jamey Grosser started producing

Popcorn Sutton's Tennessee White Whiskey supposedly using a recipe obtained from the Smoky Mountains moonshiner before his death. Hank Williams, Jr. is one of the investors. The company's website proudly claims its lineage from the crusty blockader, "Celebrating the legacy of a whiskey-making legend, we're proud to bring you Popcorn Sutton's Tennessee White Whiskey exactly the way Popcorn made it."

While Piedmont, Ole Smoky, Troy & Sons, and the Popcorn folks are turning out thousands of gallons of their moonshine every week, the operation that perhaps most harkens to the traditional corn liquor craftsman in the Great Smoky Mountains is the one run by Western North Carolina natives Cody Bradford and Chivous Downey. Both share deep family traditions in the moonshine business. The two produce their Howling Moon Mountain Moonshine in a residential area in the working-class Asheville suburb of Woodfin using cornmeal stone ground at the water-powered Dellinger Grist Mill in Mitchell

A change in North Carolina law has been a catalyst for a new generation of distillers and distilleries in the Asheville area. Featured here is Howling Moon Distillery, left to right, Chivous Downey, Bluegrass legend Raymond Fairchild, and Cody Bradford.

County. Howling Moon ferments their mash in oak barrels, uses an oak thump keg, and runs their liquor through a copper worm, although Bradford is re-conditioning an old copper condenser he discovered in his grandfather's barn. Bradford and Downey receive spokesperson services and professional advice from legendary bluegrass banjo picker and moonshiner Raymond Fairchild, a former neighbor of Popcorn Sutton's in Maggie Valley.

These legal producers, and the unknown numbers of illegal producers—from those operating huge, gas-fired Cosby Silver Clouds, to folks pursuing the family tradition, to curious types with a stove-top rig purchased over the internet—maintain an important regional institution. The epitaphs written by many observers in recent years for moonshine and the moonshiner in the Smokies were definitely premature. Indeed, the moonshine business in this region did not die alongside Popcorn Sutton in that Ford Fairlane. Far from his being the proverbial "last one," Popcorn helped usher in a new era for the iconic product. As always, the business of modern day moonshiners is a response to ever-changing economic and social conditions in the region, but far from being a dying art, the moonshine business is alive and well in the Great Smoky Mountain region.

NOTES

This little book is primarily a synthesis of original scholarship done by others and I would be remiss if I did not acknowledge my debt. The scholarly works of Wilbur Miller (*Revenuers and Moonshiners: Enforcing Federal Liquor Law in the Mountains South*—UNC Press, 1991), Bruce Stewart (*Moonshiners and Prohibitionists: The Battle Over Alcohol in Southern Appalachia*—U. of Kentucky Press, 2011), W. J. Rorabaugh (*The Alcoholic Republic: An American Tradition*—Oxford U. Press, 1981), and Charles Thompson (*Spirits of Just Men: Mountaineers, Liquor Bosses, and Lawmen in the Moonshine Capital of the World*—U. Of Illinois Press, 2011) were crucial in both providing context and key details of the history of corn liquor in the Smokies. My colleague Erica Abrams-Locklear introduced me to Elizabeth Engelhardt's work on women moonshiners in *A Mess of Greens: Southern Gender and Southern Food* (UGA Press, 2011) which added a previously unexplored component to this work. Popular works by Joseph Earl Dabney (*Mountain Moonshine* and *More Mountain Moonshine*—Bright Mountain Books), Alex Gabbard (*Return to Thunder Road: The Story Behind the Legend*—GP Press), and the students and teachers at Rabun Gap Nacoochee School who researched the first *Foxfire Book* (Anchor Books) added many anecdotes and interviews to advance the story, particularly on the 20th century.

Works on individual communities in the Smokies were also extremely helpful, including those of Elizabeth Powers and Mark Hannah (*Cataloochee: Lost Settlement of the Smokies*—Powers-Hannah), Duane Oliver (*Hazel Creek: From Then till Now*), Durwood Dunn

(*Cades Cove: The Life and Death of a Southern Appalachian Community, 1818-1937*—UT Press, 1988), and A. Randolph Shields (*The Cades Cove Story*—GSMNHA, 1981). I am especially indebted to Claudia Konker for her unpublished work on Cosby—on deposit in the Archives at Great Smoky Mountains National Park—that compiles dozens of interviews with local residents. Of course, everyone who does research on the Smokies—especially on moonshine in the region—benefits tremendously from the pioneering work of Horace Kephart in *Our Southern Highlanders*.

I must also express my deep appreciation to Annette Hartigan for her collection of so many important materials and for her research support as archivist/librarian at the GSMNP Archives and Library. I am also indebted to individuals who read parts of this work and offered valuable insights and suggestions including Erica Abrams-Locklear, Richard Starnes, Geoff Cantrell, Bill Hart, Kent Cave, Tim Silver, Brooks Blevins, and David Perry.

Many thanks are also due to my sons Sully and Coulter, my daughters Anna Clare and Taylor, and my wife Lydia for their continuous patience, support, and encouragement. I know my mother, Archie Pierce, has struggled with coming to grips with the subject matter of this book, but I so much appreciate her undying support.

Finally, I want to acknowledge the long-term influence of my academic mentors in shaping this work. The late Grady McWhiney first inspired my interest in the history of ordinary Southerners and recognized and encouraged talents and possibilities in me that I myself did not see. Forrest McDonald taught me how to write and I'll never forget the impact on my self-confidence of his words "damn well written" inscribed on a draft of my M.A. thesis. James C. Cobb helped expand and refine my interest in Southern culture, improved my writing immeasurably, and continues to inspire and encourage me. As he has done on practically every piece of my published writing, Paul Bergeron put on his editor's hat, read over this entire manuscript, kept me from embarrassing myself, and made this a much better work.

Given their salutary impact on my life and career, and the at least passing acquaintance each has had with moonshine and the culture that produced it, this book is dedicated to the memory of Dr. McWhiney and in honor of Drs. McDonald, Cobb, and Bergeron.

Photo Credits: Cody Bradford—100; Don Dudenbostel—95; Great Smoky Mountains Nationl Park Archives—4, 14, 17, 26, 31, 37, 41, 48, 58, 67, 70, 74, 75, 77, 82-83, 84, 86, 89, 90, 105; The Kephart Collection—22, 53; Bill Lea—11, 43; Vernon Lix—98 (The Bakers); Ole Smoky Tennessee Moonshine Distillery—98 (jar); D.H. Ramsey Library Special Collections, UNC Asheville—35, 81.

INDEX